MW00799823

Transform Your Emotional DNA!

"Understanding The Blueprint Of Your Life"

Author: Theresa Dale, Ph.D., N.D.

Library of Congress Catalogue Number 96-90408
ISBN #0-9652947-6-5

Published by:
The Wellness Center for Research and Education, Inc.
13050 San Vicente Blvd., Suite 206, Los Angeles, CA. 90049
Phone: 310-656-7117 / Fax: 310-656-7112

Printed in Canada

"*Transform* Your Emotional DNA"
is dedicated to the evolution of mankind
and the attainment of unconditional love on the planet.

Transform Your Emotional DNA!

Table Of Contents

Introduction
Healing with the Resonance of Love

The concept of having an *emotional DNA* may be new to you. "Your Emotional DNA" will give you a new understanding of the role your genetic blueprint plays in your life. The DNA contains a universe of information invisible to the conscious mind. This information can heal us or kill us.

The resonance of love is a powerful component of our genetic blueprint. Love is an innate response that overflows from each cell. It is a magnificent healing tool we may use to assist humanity. How does it work for creating wellness? Unconditional love is a transformational energy! With intention this energy can focus like a laser beam to create a shift in the enlightenment of the planet. Just imagine -- thousands of people focusing unconditional love on a particular area of the world. Now, do not start thinking your love is not powerful enough to shift *your* life or worrying about how could it possibly shift one entire geographical location? Your unconditional love can shift everything in your universe. The key is, it has to be unconditional. The magic of unconditional love exists in all of us.

Dare you open the door to the feeling of unconditional love? You say you feel vulnerable? That's temporary. The vulnerability shifts to security and strength when you direct the feeling of love outside yourself, resulting in a loss of all related inhibitions. Let me tell you truthfully, unconditional love is an incredible feeling whether you are on the receiving or the giving end. One thing is for sure, you cannot fake it. The shocking truth is, you can fake feeling an orgasm easier than you can fake feeling unconditional love -- or so I have been told. You see, unconditional love is a feeling, not a thought or attitude. If you try thinking about unconditional love it's not going to translate into a feeling. Unconditional love either radiates from your being, out into your environment or it does not. People who are around you, either feel the emanation of unconditional love inner peace brings or they do not.

When you were a child, you did not care about the color of someone's skin. You were in awe of them because of the feeling you got from being around them. You felt what they felt. Your love was unconditional. Conditional love is a learned response based on the emotion "fear." What is the best way to access the resonance of unconditional love? First, have a good sense of humor about your life and yourself. Lighten up! As you start loving yourself unconditionally, it becomes natural to love others unconditionally. Oh, so you think unconditional loving is a "New Age" thing. I am so glad this so-called "New Age" is bringing with it a "New Awareness" to our lives. An awareness bringing forth the understanding that we have many choices available to us.

The feeling of love is an energy that travels on an electromagnetic wave. When one resists loving unconditionally, healing is blocked. One of my patients asked me the following question, "I really love my boyfriend unconditionally but I get irritated when he doesn't do what he promised. Does that mean I don't love him unconditionally?". Unconditionally loving someone does not mean that you are going to have to give your power away. It means you love another and part of that love is you communicate your feelings and thereby bring about resolution and alignment. You can unconditionally love a person, but choose not to live with them. It's a matter of choice, not right or wrong. I believe there may be appropriate times for demonstrating *tough* unconditional love.

Doubts And Creation

Since you own the key to unleashing the most profound healing technique in the universe, why do you continue to doubt your own abilities to self-heal? Are you seeking the truth about your wellness or just an answer which is plausible? Perhaps you just want someone to give you a glimmer of hope so you can keep going. Instead you come up short. Having reached that dead end street, you become open to almost anything, as long as the answer comes from someone seemingly more powerful, representing authority. Standing at that crossroads, longing for wholeness and the return to optimum health you feel confused, still not sure of the right path. Yet, you know you do not want to spend the next 5, 10 or perhaps even 20 years in therapy or perfecting some promised path to enlightenment. Our society wants everything in an instant, particularly results. Yet, when it comes to your health you give someone else the responsibility of your healing. Sometimes you may even gamble with your life, trusting someone to cut or burn the problem out of your body. You have forgotten that you are a powerful being and no longer a helpless child needing parenting. So, stop making someone else responsible for your wellness. They are not your parent. I have had many patients who gave their power away by accepting a so-called authority point of view as *fact* -- all because they feared the outcome of their own decision. What is your fear of decisions about, anyway? Could it be that you might be wrong? Do you feel you are not educated enough to make health related decisions or to, God forbid, diagnose yourself? Isn't there a law against self-diagnosing, yet? After all, it's legal to know where your organs are located in your body. Of course, to avoid being wrong you always have the option of unconsciously allowing others to perform drastic medical procedures. Could it be that you fear responsibility? Surely you must know of others who are more of an authority about you and your body than you are? How absurd!

Lets take a realistic look at what you would need to learn to activate your innate healing power. Start with love, add a smidgen of anatomy and physiology, a pinch of good nutrition, a "Cosmic Instruction Manual" and a tool kit. This is the manual you never got upon entering earth. It will teach you how to run your universe and heal yourself in the process. The manual contains all the tools you need to become your own authority. Isn't it time to embrace your power? Let go of self-imposed limitations and empower the very essence of your innate fundamental character. It may not be instant, but then again, **you** could create it so. As all manuals, the "Cosmic Instruction Manual" begins with simple instructions, unless, your manual was designed and transcribed in the Orient. Luckily, you can get the "Cosmic Instruction Manual" in your native language. It begins with the understanding of a simple model. This model begins with a blueprint. The blueprint contains a picture of our entire physical, mental and emotional make-up.

Look at the ears. On the ears you will find acupuncture points connected to every organ, the gland, the spine, the head and the brain. The study and treatments of the ear acupuncture points are called "Auricular Therapy". The eye can also be used as a diagnostic map for the entire body, this is called "Iridology". In addition, the tongue, the teeth, the hands, the feet, and the head have their own identical blueprint of our entire physical body. Look at the teeth. There is an energetic connection between teeth, to an acupuncture meridian, a vertebra on the spine, an organ and so forth. Some European doctors consider each tooth to be an energetic extension of an organ. Studying and utilizing these mapping systems provides my patients with an accurate assessment of their overall blueprint. You can easily see how the word "blueprint" applies to various areas of the body and each cells' DNA.

Our cells contain a memory - an intelligence. This intelligence is part of the genetic coding or blueprints lying deep in the DNA. What is stored in the DNA? Information about you. Your physical and genetic features, along with disease and behavioral patterns, are part of the genetic coding. In addition, the memories of all significant programming, events from the time of birth, are an integral part of the blueprint. Visualize the DNA as a macrocosm, a universe. Your universe!

My love for humanity pushed me forward, giving me the fortitude to conduct intensive research with healing frequencies. This research eventually gave birth to the invention of a macro system that defines and develops new medical models. After years of studying the resonant numerical frequencies of organs, glands and acupuncture meridians; I had the realization that emotions and belief systems have frequencies, too. Using myself as a guinea pig whenever possible, I discovered that resisting or trying to stop the natural flow of any emotion, even love, creates emotional and physical stress frequencies. My research lead to the hypothesis that genes carry socio-cultural information that can be transformed.

Intuition And Healing

Remember the Chernobyl catastrophe and the radiation that ensued, poisoning so many people back in 1986? Well, I was vehemently against nuclear power and the transport of nuclear waste, expressing my viewpoint on radio and television. Here is a perfect demonstration showing that whatever you resist in life, you attract. I had been studying in Germany, precisely at the time of the Chernobyl incident and somehow managed to be in every city where it rained. The RADS were quickly being drawn to the ground by the rain and soon entered the food and water. Before I was even aware of what was happening, my knees swelled to twice their normal size. Simultaneously I experienced fatigue and candida symptoms. Even walking was painful. I knew that only I could get myself into a mess like this and only I could get myself out of it. Radiation poisoning, now there's a challenge! Cure myself or die. Or possibly face a bone marrow transplant. Just the thought of these alternatives was horrifying.

My intuition told me to take Magentum 10 M, (a high potency homeopathic remedy made from the color magenta), Cesium 10 M and Phytolacca 12 C, (a low potency homeopathic remedy made from Poke-Root used to drain the radiation out). Within hours I noticed a difference and then within a few days of taking the homeopathic remedies, the swelling in my knees greatly lessened. I was relieved that there was a speedy sign of healing. A complete healing took about a year.

Needless to say, I learned a lesson from this experience. The great intuitive "Ah-Ha", light bulb had been lit. I had created all these health problems just so I could subsequently cure them, thereby enabling myself to identify with the feeling "I was a great doctor". This of course gave me a tremendous sense of self-worth where there was a lack. It helped me feel like a person who could really be of benefit to society.

There's A Movie In Your Cells!

This awareness convinced me that I no longer needed to create any physical illness to prove my worth. The only way to change this old pattern was to locate the identity and release it, changing this pattern at the cellular level. I knew what needed to be done, but like so many of you, I didn't know how to proceed. The blueprint of my life was like a movie with a definite script and plot. The plot was self-destruction. I explored one technique after another, looking for a way to change my blueprint and achieve an unencumbered state of happiness. I experienced some benefit from these techniques I embraced, but the results were not permanent. It was from this research I was able to create magnificent healing tools. As a result of exploring the many different medical modalities and processes necessary to create these tools, I eliminated the identities that were controlling my destiny.

The Road Has Many Paths

A person may be considered "therapy resistant", - - any therapies tried will fail to bring about a permanent healing. Why does one type of therapy produce a miracle for one person and has no effect at all on another? The following case history may lead you to your answer.

A male patient, late 50's, was diagnosed by traditional medicine with lymphoma. He was my patient for three months and was healing very quickly. The swelling in his left side, including his neck, was 75% less swollen. His white blood count was normal and holding.   Months of blood tests agreed with the results from the NeuroPhysical Reprogramming testing   (see Chapter 9).   Yet, the patient was very resistant to achieving a total state of wellness, either physically or emotionally. In other words, he definitely did not relish the idea of experiencing any negative emotions. He continued following the traditional medical model, making it "the" authority, even though this was standing in the way of his recovery. He was frightened. He let the authorities put the fear of God in to him. It's a known fact that fear lowers the immune system. Even my telling him this could not embrace the fact that he could cure himself. So, he refused to follow my recommendations and explore his emotional state. Although his diet was fairly clean, his disease progressed. What makes a person resistant to total wellness? Perhaps, it's an inner spiritual desire to move on, to drop the physical body. That is at least one viewpoint. Another is, that the culprit running the show is an **identity**. I have assisted other patients in their wellness who were diagnosed with cancer by their personal physician. The difference between one cancer patient experiencing a cure and another not experiencing a cure, is not the type of cancer, but the level one has of unconscious and conscious resistance. Which path in the road will you take?

Let's take a look at the emotion despair, as a source of illness. According to the Five Element Theory of Acupuncture despair corresponds to the stomach. When you resist feeling despair, it is stored in the stomach until it is experienced and released. The feeling and state of despair is stimulated by an identity who is acting out a role. The identity will temporarily prevent you from tuning into the inner peace that is eternally present. Even though it is invisible to you, its existence is like a huge storm cloud blocking out the warmth of the sun.

Your Body Is Like An Antenna

Your body has an electromagnetic field that serves as an antenna. The body attracts, stores and receives information. Since wellness is a state of mind and being, you have the unlimited ability to attract wellness and abundance into your life. Why do we then create pain and disease? Mysterious as it sounds, we attract the exact frequency we emit. We attract the reflection of who we think we are and what we think we deserve. For instance, when thoughts run rampant in our head, we can easily create a reality filled with drama.

You have a purpose in life. You are a spiritual being and have a right to be here and prosper. You are on earth for your own evolution and experience. In order to experience the things you want, you must consciously and with determination, decide to be responsible for all aspects of your life. Otherwise, your identities greatly influence the type of experiences you create.

Your unconscious mind can create a diversion in your life causing you to "check out" and become unaware of the blockages in your own evolutionary process. You may think you've been forgotten or misplaced, you may feel your path is mysterious and deeply hidden. The result of this thinking is you avoid evolution. I have personally experienced this in my life and I know of countless others who consistently either "get sick" or express a need to "fall in love" in order to feel something. Often that feeling creates drama, which resulting in either physical or emotional pain. These behaviors go back to our earliest years when we were not allowed to experience life from our own unique perspective. You viewed aspects of your life through an identity's eyes, filtering out many opportunities to expand your viewpoint.

If you have a war going on in the core of your being, it may be caused by a dissonant identity creating a dichotomy, or love-hate relationship. This sets up a pattern of confusion. Confusion keeps you in a state of non-evolution and avoidance.

Even a healthy, aware and growth-oriented person can become stuck. When inertia takes over you can become frustrated and anxious. These emotions are fear-based survival mechanisms, manifesting from the need to hold onto your viewpoints. They become blocks that keep you from evolving, from becoming "self-actualized", and from your inherent wellness. Releasing the core of these blocks will enable you to experience your inner power and vision, allowing the healing of your body, mind and soul. By connecting to your innate cellular intelligence, this inner "seeing" manifests effortlessly. As your awareness of this connection grows, you start to feel enthusiasm for life. The passion and enthusiasm create momentum for bringing new forms into being, and a new reality emerges.

"It's so simple a child can do it." In fact children do it automatically, feeling the enthusiasm of each moment. Simple, yes, but not so easy. Many people have forgotten how. Remember the magical times of your childhood, you were in love with all you were doing and seeing. Time often felt as if it was standing still. You had the presence and the ability to focus on one little toy or one task or one person. But many of you have buried this ability under experiences of trauma and stress, in other words.....drama. It's still there, skill you possessed as a child, and you can recreate the magic again by loving as a child would; purely and innocently. For me, there is only one kind of love, one way to love. To love like a child - unconditionally. Other feelings are labeled "love" because we all desire being "in love". You see, the label feels good. So, using it is an expression of emotion and caring. Perhaps appreciation. Unconditional love, I believe is the true force behind the awesome energy called God.

Children naturally express their emotions and fears.   Laughter, crying and screaming are built in release mechanisms that are healthy. Yet, during childhood you were taught to stop these natural release processes. You learned to hold in your emotions. As you moved into adulthood, you became afraid, afraid to express yourself, and afraid to be judged childish.   I love to feel all of my emotions, after all, that's a great part of what healed me. If someone thinks I'm childish - great! They are obviously thinking too much. I enjoy being childlike.

Let go of other people's expectations of you. Enthusiasm and excitement are the first keys to this process. Certainty perpetuates the feeling of "knowing", which in turn, immediately ignites the creative force within you. If you continue a new pattern for seven days, it gives momentum to your efforts. Integrating this pattern into your life for a few months gives birth to a new matrix you can keep for the rest of your life, if *you* choose.

Many feelings that block your momentum, stem from a belief in the expectation of catastrophe. The expectation of catastrophe is shared in mass consciousness. Fear is the frequency that attracts catastrophe. So, embrace your fears and you will take away the reflection. Now, all you have to do is release the identity who is feeling the fear. This will make a profound difference in the reality you experience. When the old patterns are released, there is an immediate stimulation and integration of new cellular electro-chemical connections. In other words, you develop a transcendent awareness, which you actually feel as a new part of you.

VIII

Chapter 1
The Anatomy Of An Illness
(and other life conditions)

The anatomy of an illness begins with an identity. An identity is a character or a sub-personality that takes on various visible and invisible shapes, forming an energy pattern. This identity may be genetic, containing within itself beliefs and emotions. Like a character in a movie, this identity plays a role in your life. Your character and your belief system mold the experiences of your life. This persona's whisperings spawn your beliefs and emotions, at times shouting to challenge your notions of who you are and how you should relate to your world.

Your cellular memory absorbs this identity and stores it until it is discovered, experienced and then released. The identity is invisible because it resides in the realm of the unconscious and asserts itself by manifesting life experiences and conditions. When you release an emotion or belief, (symptoms), without knowing the causal factor, (identity), the energy pattern will continue unbroken. The pattern continues to result in emotional and physical conditions.

Patients tell me they are afraid of how they will be judged if they express anger. They fear, at worst, hurting someone, or at least making a fool of themselves. When a person is angry, they radiate this emotion so intensely others feel the heat. There is a way to release anger without hurting someone else. Try this the next time you feel angry, stop for a moment and deeply feel the anger in your body, breathe through the anger, and like magic, the intensity will lift. Next, communicate your feelings. When you resist feeling an emotion you give it power. When you feel anger, you are actually feeling an identity's anger.

There exist both positive and negative identities. The positive identities serve us in life affirming ways while the negative identities cast shadows over our emotional health. By using specific tools undesirable identities can be removed. Begin learning about changing these identities by using the Reality Shifting Exercise.

What is a belief?

A belief is an idea, a conviction, an unshakable truth manifesting itself into a reality. As individuals we perceive truth based on our belief systems. Since identities are attached to beliefs, a belief is symptomatic of an existing identity. Identities create your reality. A reality is any experience of an event, emotion or life condition. This includes physical and mental disease: a reality is anything you experience as being true.

"Sex is dangerous." How about, "I am going to burn myself out if I don't change my schedule" or "Relationships are difficult"? These are examples of beliefs, conscious or unconscious, contained within an identity. They have the potential to create and result in our experiencing beliefs as truths. "My parents will never change", "Life is a struggle", "Nothing works for me", "My mother had breast cancer, maybe I'll get it too", "Everyone my age has wrinkles and health problems", "I'm not enough"...I'm sure you get the idea. Generations pass along some pretty nifty beliefs and identities, don't you think?

An Emotion Is A Symptom!

In my research I have discovered one identity may contain many beliefs. One belief may stimulate 20 or more emotions. Therefore, it is vital to discover which identity is creating which belief. Without this knowledge a person endlessly struggles with the same emotions because they never truly go away. Unfortunately, merely locating and releasing emotions without eliminating the identify holding them in place will mean on going therapy. A chronic emotional pattern; like a pain, a cough or a headache, is just a symptom and not the root of a problem. An identity and its belief system cause the struggles and sufferings in life. The key to discovering the root of behavioral patterns, disharmony or illness is in examining any chronic emotional pattern. You may work on emotions your entire life and forever feel stuck because life does not flow.

The Cause And Effect Of Faulty Belief Systems And Identities.

Why do belief systems remain intact throughout our adult life time? Where do they spring from? We've known since childhood and possibly before, that beliefs reside in each cell trapped as information. They are a part of your blueprint, a part of yourself. As such their invisibility leaves you to believe in them as truths, "that's just the way I am -- I can't change." Now, this is a belief -- isn't it?

When you find yourself resistant to change, an identity may be the cause. There is a tendency to blame others for your emotional upsets. As you take responsibility for creating your own emotions, you will be giving birth to a new identity. Through this new identity you will gain a new perspective. No one and no thing can make you feel an emotion not there already.

A case history nicely illustrating this point is that of a 48 year old woman who, because of her belief system, looked 32 years old. Not only was her face without signs of aging, but her body was youthful. Mentally and physically she created a gorgeous physical self. She shared with me how other women and members of her own family felt uncomfortable around her because of her appearance. To be accepted by others she unconsciously created the symptoms of menopause, complete with hot flashes. Initially, she told me she believed she had slowed down the aging process. I felt she had a hard time coping with the truth, the truth being she had *almost* accomplished her goal. A method of kinesiological testing I had developed detected plenty of resistance around the issue of "getting old". I invited her to discover the character or identity inside her that felt old and aging. She admitted she felt guilty and ashamed of how uncomfortable she was making others feel. I encouraged her to go deeper into that feeling. As she did she found that *she* was uncomfortable, yet in awe, of her young looks. We eliminated the identity that felt uncomfortable. The guilt and shame ceased to exist when the character/identity dissolved. Then her menopausal symptoms stopped. Now you're wondering about this whole area of menopause and hormone replacement therapy. Natural hormone replacement is an alternative issue when locating and releasing the identity that believes it's a "victim of time".

Every Identity Creates An Experience.

 Consider this: Your childhood very likely included seemingly constant criticism from your parents. You probably felt misunderstood when forced to cope with the emotions, ideals and judgments of your parents. When you got sick, your parents would take you to see a doctor who routinely answered with a shot or pill. Making it impossible for the true cause of your discomfort or illness to be discovered. What were you feeling before the illness? The emotion you tried so hard not to feel burdened your immune system. At that time in your life you did not have a choice or maybe you felt you did not have the *right* to make a choice? You believed someone else was responsible for your wellness, your happiness. Let's face it, you were influenced by your parents' values, both positively and negatively. Maybe your parents did not have a tool kit either. Whatever the reason, their attempts to teach you their idea of success and happiness did not work for you. Your soul had a different expression. Your childhood environment caused you to either follow in your parents' footsteps or rebel. Perhaps you never allowed your soul's expression to develop, because you never set down your own rules and values. Some of us are still following our parents' rules and still other people accept rules from outside authorities because we do not know how to create our own. For some people following pre-set guidelines for a happy life seems like the easier way, despite evidence of those guidelines leading the way to disease and depression. How many times in your life have you heard "Don't make waves!" and "Do what you're told!" and accepted these same kind of rules about healing. You were undoubtedly exposed to your parents' patterning related to illness. Some of these patterns were absorbed into your cellular memory and have a direct effect on the quality of your life and health. Your parents' approach was probably the traditional one and most likely included surgery. How can health manifest itself with a program like this running your life? It blocks your own intuitive process and healing ability. Possibly, you were not empowered to trust yourself as a child. It is truly a wonder we are able to retain any of our sanity and vision to see through these illusions. Some of us transform in spite of it all. Knowing who we are, we prosper, while others are still searching for the truth. The TRUTH? There is only your truth, you create it from knowing your essence.

4

It may seem like I'm painting a dark picture of childhood and parenting. Not so. However, I do feel that our society needs to devise a way to stop bringing unwanted children into a world of abuse and abandonment. In a society where a license is required to get married, why not require a license in order to parent or better yet, require training for parents to better care for their children? Our society is currently transforming. Awareness of children's special needs is growing and parenting is changing for the better. Less than a decade ago, hitting children was not considered abuse. Now, thanks to the media, our awareness of the depth of child abuse issues has risen.

Many parents experience their childhood as a painful, traumatic experience. They hope to evolve past their parents' performance. My patients who are parents express fears of emotionally harming their children due to their own behavioral patterns. Some parents change their identities and belief systems so their dysfunctional patterns will not be passed on to their children. Others deny the pain, choosing to remember the joy of happy times. Still, other parents pay so much attention to the dark side of childhood, it overshadows the light. For many others, the light side is non-existent.

Without the tools to evolve you are going to spend a large part of your life settling for whatever comes your way, instead of realizing many of your dreams. Assuming full responsibility for your life and experiences will create movement in your life. Stop being a victim; blaming your parents, the universe and God. I urge you to experience all aspects of the resisted darkness residing deep within yourself. Only then can you finally heal and feel the light. With the light comes the gift of unconditional love -- for yourself and others.

Identities Are Morphogenetic.

An identity, whether positive or negative, is morphogenetic in nature. Breaking down the word morphogenetic we gain a clearer understanding of the word's meaning. "Ology" means the study of something and "morpho" means form, shape or structure, so morphology means the study of form, shape or structure. Genetics is the study of hereditary traits in living organisms. Therefore "morphogenetic" means the study of structural development in organisms. It studies the characteristic forms of embryos and developing systems responsible for organizing the formation of material systems. An identity is an energy pattern with a form. Invisible at its conception, an identity can become visible at later stages of its existence. It may develop into the form of a physical disease. This shaped form is responsible for the organization, structure and creation of all experience. My research confirms that the blueprint in your DNA is a holographic pattern. The blueprint in every cell creates itself time and again in the same form, because it is morphogenetic in nature. Within each blueprint are many energy patterns containing numerous identities. As I mentioned before, these identities also contain beliefs which together can be passed on genetically from one generation to the next, until they are finally released.

Genetic Disease Patterns

In terms of physics, every disease has a frequency range. When I speak about frequencies I am referring to Hertz (Hz). One hertz = a unit of frequency, equal to one cycle per second. This was discovered by the German Physicist H. Hertz, 1857-1894. In addition each organ, gland and acupuncture meridian resonates to a specific band width of Hz frequencies when health exists. The correspondence of frequencies to organs and meridians was researched by a German medical doctor, Dr. Reinholdt Voll. An identity that is sabotaging your life in some way alters the normal healthy frequency of an organ to an unhealthy or disharmonic frequency. If the identity and its emotions are resisted, the identity's energy pattern will be trapped in the organ in accordance to the resisted emotion. The organ may not exhibit symptoms for many years. Then one day, a pain arises. You ask, "Where did that come from?". If at the core of the pain or symptom the identity is not eliminated, then it's possible to pass this ticking time bomb on to a beloved child.

An energy pattern can be made up of one or more identities, each producing multiple frequencies. Obviously when dealing with several emotions, all occurring simultaneously, you have multiplied the number of frequencies, creating a very chaotic state. In a case like this, there could be a large number of identities stimulating the emotional upset.

6

An explanation for the occurrence of a so-called "genetic disease pattern", is that a disease pattern is the result of identities and the attached beliefs captured in the DNA of our cells. Making it impossible for us to create and achieve what we want out of life. In a case like this the attainment of good health could remain blocked for part or all of your life. I'm sure you've heard of people dying from a heart attack at the same age as their father or mother. The energy pattern causing the heart attack resides in the heart for an entire lifetime, until a certain biological age and then, like a lit fuse, there is an explosion. This holds equally true when an identity's energy pattern includes beliefs resulting in the person feeling "unsuccessful" or "unlucky" in life. You see, the identity's energy pattern and frequency blocks the manifestation of your goals by acting as a filter allowing only certain experiences to exist in your personal universe. Therefore it's easy to see how like a magnet you attract certain types of experiences and not others.

Visualize a blueprint or map. The map contains genetic coding for your physical features; the color of your eyes, your hair or your skin. The information in the blueprint is not limited to physical attributes. The DNA contains emotional and behavioral patterns, the genetic historical data making up a large part of your personality. Our cells' DNA coding can be compared to the way a computer stores information on its hard drive. Meaning the parents' identities are capable of storing feelings of low self-esteem not only for themselves, but also for their children. Likewise, any identity storing feelings of optimism or success can pass these qualities on to succeeding generations, because the cells store the identity, the identity is stored in the cell.

How do identities become stuck in our cells in the first place? They become stuck when we *resist* feeling our emotions. This occurs on a conscious or unconscious level. It is ludicrous to think that you have your parents' and grandparents' physical attributes coded in your DNA's blueprint, but not their behavioral patterns. The good news is you can change disease patterns and life conditions. You must act on your desire to change. I have personally experienced a child born with Downs Syndrome, who transformed this condition. Along with a change in the child's appearance, there was a change in the child's ability to learn and grow emotionally. Once this is understood and integrated into your personal consciousness, this knowledge will serve as a model of hope leading you to the experience of transformation. By ceasing to analyze WHY this child was healed and how these results are possible, you can stop wasting precious time and begin spending it on healing yourself.

Attachment

Attachment causes emotional pain, stemming from an identity holding onto the past. You do not need to drag the past around anymore, unless you're somehow served by an identity thriving on pain and suffering. Emotional pain experienced in relationships is created from our own ideas and beliefs. The expectations you have of others cause you pain, forming an attachment to an unpleasant outcome. A sure fire way to create an experience falling short of your hoped for expectation, is to be in reality *attached* to a particular outcome. Attachment is a dependency on something or someone.

When you react to a situation or event, "the same old way", you are reinforcing old patterns. This means familiar situations will manifest the same outcomes over and over again. You are then living out the sum total of *your* previous choices. How do you start empowering yourself? You start by eliminating past concepts and belief systems. Anything no longer serving you must go. This includes expectations and judgments. Then establish new goals.

If The Past Doesn't Exist -- Why Do People Have Chronic Illness?

All illness reflects the presence of an identity keeping the illness in a state of continual recreation. You are dragging the identity and concept of illness along with you from your past into your present. For example, a belief or a judgment like, "Cancer is incurable", might keep you stuck in a creation of illness and contribute to the onset of cancer. Still more dangerous are beliefs like, "I can't heal myself, but others can do it for me" or the most insidious of all, "I get more attention when I am sick".

If you believe, just because an authority tells you, that you'll contract breast cancer because your mother or grandmother suffered from the disease, then you open yourself up to a greater probability of creating the disease within yourself. You do not have to believe this possibility on a conscious level! Wallowing in the past from moment to moment, year to year, you'll rob yourself of the joy of experiencing life in the present. What is the first step in letting go of the past? Get out of your head. Yes, stop the mental processes resulting in disease and depression. Don't worry you won't go stupid, you'll just stop the drama-go-round. This is a good first step since our ideas and beliefs have a bad habit of playing over and over in our minds and a quiet mind will be a welcomed relief.

Inner Communication -- Inner Power

Of tantamount importance is clear, honest and direct communication with yourself. Only then can you take responsibility for all you experience. Let me explain. Many people feel by taking responsibility for what we experience we're making reservations for a future guilt trip. No need place to blame the universe, on yourself or on anyone for that matter. In my view, taking responsibility is laying claim to your power. When you stop blaming others, you eliminate the victim "identity".

Go get a mirror. Look yourself straight in the eyes and see yourself healed. One of my favorite expressions is: "If I created it -- I can discreate it". This my friends is truly a feeling of freedom. Want to try it? Repeat this phrase over and over, soon, with practice it will roll off your tongue -- and then it happens. You realize you are free.

Here's a good way to produce harmony in your day. Start your day by closing your eyes and breathing slowly and deeply. Connect your breaths. Be careful, because if your breathing remains shallow you may hyperventilate, so keep breathing slowly, deeply and rhythmically. After deep breathing for a minute or two, focus a feeling of love in to your heart area and feel the warmth. If you analyze what you're feeling, you'll shift out of the feeling and shut down the experience. Feel the love enter all of your cells, beginning with your toes and spreading to the top of your head. Feel the inner peace.

Mind Games

Being an intellectual does not mean you have to stay stuck in your own head. "Going mental", can be a hiding place. Hiding within your own intellect can be a way of avoiding your feelings. Choosing a brilliant disguise and confining yourself within the identity of an intellectual expresses a chronic need to be the center of attention. This character obsessively needs to feel he or she is "right" at all times. Instead of feeling your life, you are thinking about your life. Remember, there is no freedom in intellect. True wisdom grows and flowers within our intuition, not our mental processes.

Have you ever wondered what it would be like to be stupid? I had a huge resistance about being "stupid" at one point in my life, so I decided to embrace it and explore this identity. At first I was fearful I might stay stupid, then I realized this too was childhood programming. So, I deliberately created a "stupid" identity and experienced life through a new perspective. Once the resistance to being "stupid" dissolved, I automatically shifted out of the identity. Looking back on my "stupid" identity, I remember feeling utterly blissful. Maybe that's where the old saying comes from, "ignorance is bliss".

Your truth will emerge from living your life, not analyzing it. When you analyze life, you put everything at a distance and force yourself to judge every single aspect of life in a right or wrong context. Perhaps your strongest belief is in your own limitations? Our most powerful tool is our intuition. When we endlessly over analyze things, we suppress our intuition. This can become an addiction that keeps us from feeling, inhibiting our natural intuition. In an holistic sense, anyone who is free of these self-imposed limitations will be capable of allowing the interaction between cell and spirit to take place in an harmonious way. Experiencing freedom in the intellect lasts only for the duration of a thought, true freedom lies in establishing peace between all the opposites within yourself.

Try looking at life this way. There are three universes; yours, mine, and rest of the world's. What I experience in my universe will not be experienced the same way by someone else in their universe. Consciously or unconsciously, the things we align set up the experiences we have in our universe. Therefore, if we have absorbed and integrated an identity from a parent who believes himself or herself to be a victim, we *will* become a victim. If we make the decision to instill peace and harmony in ourselves, then, even though there is mass consciousness belief to the contrary, we will manifest peace and harmony. Say you have chosen a particular reality and have not yet experienced it? You probably have doubts keeping you from manifesting this reality.

The Healthy Ego

How can anyone be so egotistical as to believe they can cure themselves or stop the aging process? That's ridiculous. Even though the phenomenon of the ego has been the object of psychoanalytic debate for centuries, I decided to view it from another perspective. Crystallizing my awareness of the ego, I see the ego as a natural healthy form of self-esteem. On the other hand when the ego becomes asserted and forced out into the environment, the assertion itself springs from an "identity" or "character" that is focused totally on itself. When the core of a person's love remains so immature as to include only one's own reflection, this person exhibits the very definition of self-centeredness. The self-centered identity grasps a higher sense of self-esteem in order to cover up feelings of inadequacy. For example, a person who constantly asserts to others how successful he or she is, may actually be experiencing feelings of failure or the fear of failure. In order for the character to play its role and feel successful, he or she *overtly* behaves the way they would like to be perceived by others.

Unconscious identities are in everyone. We function daily by moving from one identity to another, like an actor moving from part to part. Sometimes people can become stuck in one identity and day in and day out they will not budge from that one identity. You can imagine the frustration of yearning for the experiences of being a lover, when you are locked on to the identity of a mother. Just imagine the tremendous amount of stress you expend when you remain stuck in one identity. Like being confined in a box with invisible walls, you cannot see what you are bumping into, but you know something is there holding you back. You feel a lack of movement. Being locked in any identity can keep you in a form of darkness. Once you experience and embrace the darkness, then and only then will you be free. Your dragons will transform into angels!

A Recipe For Curing Any Disease!

Mental and emotional patterning sets up a resonance which draws to us our life experiences, both positively and negatively. You see each action must account for itself in each moment. Every action has a reaction. Therefore, in your daily life it is vital before you act, to consider what kind of reaction will bear upon yourself and the universe as a whole. If you don't believe it, look around and consider the similarities between the events in your own personal universe and the world as a whole.

Being a creative powerhouse, you understand a health problem can begin by the act of resisting something. The severity of the problem is determined by how much energy is spent in this resistance. Therefore, let's say by resisting something in your life you have created a health problem for yourself. After recognizing the problem and taking responsibility for it, how do you fix it? For example, if told there is no cure and you should simply learn to live with a health problem many of us accept this advice and do nothing further -- except suffer. In this kind of situation listen to people who support your own gut instincts and never deny your own inner wisdom.   When negative emotions like anger and guilt are heaped on our immune system they only burden it, leaving it open and vulnerable to a wide range of health problems. Some are labeled colds or flu, while others are diagnosed as cancer or AIDS. Obviously the differences between a condition commonly known as a sore throat and conditions labeled cancer or AIDS revolve around the viewpoint experiencing the disease.   Your viewpoint controls how you experience life, and the way you experience disease. Remember, viewpoints come from identities. When you have harmonic or healthy identities there is no need to fear personal catastrophes occurring.

Let's take a look at four factors which influence a physical illness or life condition:

- The importance you give a disease, feeds the disease. The amount of resistance you exert against a condition attracts the same condition. This means at least one identity must be resisting.

- Fear experienced by an identity creates the condition and intensifies the symptoms.

- Negative judgements you make on yourself and the disease. Most people are not aware that by labeling a disease, they are passing **judgment** on the disease and in effect, feeding the disease. For example, when a doctor labels a disease cancer and pronounces the patient's condition life-threatening or incurable, he or she makes it more difficult to treat because the outcome is prejudged by the doctor and believed by the patient. The judgment keeps feeding the condition and in turn activates fear, which in turn suppresses the immune system. This is demonstrated

12

in the case of the disease called AIDS. The reaction to the label of AIDS ignites the resistance and makes the patient's case more difficult. Learning specific tools can dissolve the resistance, the judgment and change the label. Ignorance in our society will be replaced with unconditional love and excellence. When health practioners choose to be "partners in health" with their patients instead of trying to impersonate "almighty God", it will liberate both the doctor and the patient, resulting in a prognosis allowing for a vital and rejuvenated immune system.

- A great factor in staying healthy is learning to stop mental tapes playing in your head and learning to control your own mind.

Any of the these factors can be fueled or influenced by information received from either the media or established medical groups. I know this is a drastic step, but there are appropriate times when the television needs to be turned off and ignored.

How Do I Locate An Identity?

There are a few ways to locate an identity. The most effective way I know of, is to discover which core identity remains stuck in an organ causing problems in either the physical condition or the life situation. Then use the Meta Wellness Home Study Program or the non-invasive testing protocol, NeuroPhysical Reprogramming. Ask yourself a couple of questions; "Who would create such an experience?" or "What type of person would create this reality?". The answer to these questions will be the correct identities. You are looking for the type of identity which would hold these kinds of beliefs. You may come up with an answer that you cannot relate to immediately on a conscious level. You may even feel resistance towards the answer. I have observed in thousands of patients the more resistance felt toward a specific identity, the more likely that identity is a part of their blueprint. Trust your inner wisdom!

You will have an easier time shifting out of any negative identity you find yourself stuck in the more you understand about identities. The good news is after uncovering and eliminating a negative identity you can replace it with a new positive identity. My students ask me if they can function without identities. Being free of identities, the positive and the negative, feels as if you are having an out-of-body experience. You can neither think, nor function in the physical world.

Here's an exercise which will help you locate identities. If you have a particular pain or health problem, locate it and feel the form of the afflicted area inside your body. Then put yourself "inside" the pain. Feel the size of the pain, and ask "What are you?" In an intuitive state, wait for the answer. Do not think, FEEL. Just let it pop into your awareness. Essentially you are asking the pain what it is dramatizing. Keep repeating this process and asking, "What are you?", until you feel the charge release or the pain stop. Most likely you will gain some insight from running this simple process.

The use of over-the-counter and prescription drugs has become so widespread today that as soon as we feel something uncomfortable or different in our bodies, we want to stop it, immediately. Anti-depressants and pain killers numb you, that's why you're taking them. Drugs suppress our awareness of our identities, masking faulty belief systems and the emotions at the root of our symptoms. Even continuous long-term use of herbs and supplements, may do more damage than good. Unfortunately when prevented from feeling our pain, we are also prevented from healing ourselves. Choosing this path, denies you access to the real cellular causes of your life issues.

Forcing A Thought Out Of Your Mind Is Resistance!

Let's take a moment and reflect on this idea of your belief systems having the power to either stimulate growth or precede disease. In other words, life can grow and evolve from joy or at the other extreme, through resistance, create disease and then *hopefully* grow from that experience. With every turn, resistance keeps you stuck in old patterns.

After years spent resisting feelings, you lose touch with their existence. Eventually, if only in your own mind, you deny and bury them. Yes! Invisible, because you are unaware of the presence of the belief system and the identity.

Resistance alone creates an electromagnetic energy charge which, over time, can effect neurotransmitter production causing conditions as varied as Dyslexia,

Myasthenia Gravis, Multiple Sclerosis, Muscular Dystrophy, Alzheimer's Disease or Parkinson's Disease, just to name a few.

The way to longevity, youth or stamina is through the consistent expression of feeling. Consequently, when we resist expressing our feelings, we block the flow of life. We end up living in our own heads, reduced to merely thinking and analyzing about our lives and only experiencing suffering, fatigue, and exhaustion.

Your Immune System And Resistance!

Vulnerability to disease manifests in the human body when an individual resists feeling an emotion. This actually lowers the immune system. The more you resist a few sniffles the more likely you are to come down with a cold. After decades of resistance and denial the stakes can rise to include the possibility of cancer. Whenever you have a pain, somewhere there is a resistance to something or someone. Any resistance has the potential to lead to physical symptoms. A physical symptom is the body's way of signaling an illness is in the making. An identity contributes as a causal factor. Resistance intensifies the pain. When a doctor diagnoses a condition and you resist the diagnosis, by virtue of your resistance you are intensifying the severity of your own physical condition.

To clarify further, resistance is similar to pushing against something. It's an inner fight or put another way, your reaction to an opposing force. Any refusal to accept responsibility for an experience -- is resistance. Without intending, you are putting yourself in the role of a victim. When you blame God or the universe, you give up your power. By assuming full responsibility for your life you can fix anything. It can be like magic! The concept of you being responsible for creating your own illness or contributing to the condition of your life does not leave for any gray areas, does it? Please understand I know it feels better and safer to believe there is a gray area in the equation. However, if you want to heal a life condition or illness, the power behind creating your new reality is taking full responsibility for your part in the drama.

How do you dissolve these layers of resisted emotions and beliefs? Simply allow yourself to experience and embrace them. Then you will create a change so profound your body will actually regain balance *on a cellular level.*

If you believe someone, whoever that someone might be, when they tell you "there is no hope", you will take on that belief and manifest hopelessness. Very possibly a disease, which could easily be cured thanks to a more beneficial belief system, is allowed to continue plaguing you as you maintain the "victim" identity.

About eight years ago I assisted a 55 year old man who was diagnosed with grand mal seizures associated with epilepsy. He was told his condition was hopeless. He was preparing to have an exploratory lobotomy, (a type of extreme brain surgery), in less than a month. At this time he was told the prognosis was grim and included him possibly ending up either bed-ridden, in a coma or living as a vegetable for the rest of his life. None of the many medications his doctor prescribed had any effect in improving his condition. In fact his symptoms continued to worsen and from time to time he would black out into unconsciousness while walking home or riding the bus.

This condition left the patient unable to work for more than two years. During this inactivity he experienced periods of low self-esteem and was visibly in the throes of an overwhelming sense of hopelessness and despair. This was evidenced in the suppressed state of his immune system. For approximately four months I began to see him for one hour sessions twice a week. Later this was reduced to once a week. At each visit I would share positive information regarding his condition and give him homework, including readings to help change his beliefs. Making it clear, I told him he could cure himself if he took immediate action.

One of the things he shared with me was his fear for his father, who was in the medical field. Upon examination we discovered this condition of fear was connected with an identity locked into competing with his father's success. He had deeply buried secrets involving his relationship with his father which were torturing his mind. I assisted him in handling and understanding the fear of facing his father. In addition, I put him on a nutritional program including amino acids and high doses of magnesium. Additionally I employed magnetic field therapy. After just one month there was sufficient evidence to see this new program was working. This gave him the glimmer of hope he needed to continue with the program. In one year he had cut back to using a single medication and was back teaching at the university. His heart condition and all other symptoms abated and his perception and awareness of himself shifted due to his new identities and beliefs.

My own solid beliefs hold that for every patient's recovery his or her perception of the condition, along with the condition itself, are their own creations. If they choose to, they can eliminate them. Don't merely treat the label of a disease, remove the label and dissolve the identities.

Remember no one person or system has all the answers or knowledge necessary to discern whether a disease, mental or emotional, is incurable. No one person who touches your life can control your experiences, unless you give up your power. You have the ability to know your own answers. You are not always in the wrong and the doctor in the right. Any so-called, "authority", will have a perception and viewpoint different from your own. There is no right or wrong, only perception, a difference in viewpoints. All you need do quite simply, is trust yourself and get out of your own way, so the answers are allowed to reveal themselves.

Increasing numbers of people feel their health issues are opportunities and catalysts for growth. Our society is becoming more and more aware of healthful belief systems and techniques for healing. Accepting responsibility for our education becomes self-perpetuating. Before we know it, a new confidence and sense of worth begins to emerge. When power stops being given away the possibility of self-realization is born.

Chapter 2
Meta-Consciousness™

Life flows through you in rivers of light, streaming and pulsing through every cell of your body. This comprises your natural state, your life as it was meant to be lived, unimpeded. Feelings are a big part of the flow of life. They rise in us, swell, gush in a tremendous outpouring...and life flows. Life flows unless we resist our feelings. Resistance stops the flow of life. By letting go of resistance we acquire the key to fully experiencing life.

"Your Emotional DNA", was created to assist you in letting go of your resistance by teaching you to open up those parts of yourself shut-down a long time ago. Let yourself expand and stretch with the new information you are now clearly ready to hear. By picking up this book you proclaim your readiness. Be a giant rubber band stretching out into the universe. This is something you're capable of as you integrate the information within these pages. As you absorb the new concepts in this book do so with a lightness of being, seriousness will contract you and inhibit your ability to learn. Laughter and lightness will expand you.

Behavioral Programs Are In Meta-Consciousness!

Through researching the complexities of the human mind, I have discovered a deeper, more profound level of consciousness. Like a burial ground, consciousness contains many levels. Misguided behavioral programs lie deep, undisturbed, but never at rest. From out of nowhere, these insidious tapes suddenly start to play, humbling us once again. You might compare this level of consciousness, which I call Meta-Consciousness, to a hidden place where the master computer chip plugs in, like the hard disc on a computer. Adhering to old and often genetically inherited patterns they remain stuck in place by subconscious resistance. I liken unconscious resistance to fly-paper attracting experience equal to the amount of resistance.

While at home one evening, the word "Meta-Consciousness" flew through my mind.

Being intrigued by the newness of the word I sat down at my computer to see what would happen. As if a channel had blown open to another dimension, information poured out of me as soon as I began. Soon it was revealed to me that Meta-Consciousness is a level of consciousness accessed through the achievement of a brain wave state deeper than the relaxation level of Delta. Meta-Consciousness contains the more historic parts of the unconscious cellular memory and can be accessed through the NeuroPhysical Reprogramming protocol which is taught in the Wellness Course II.

The Key to Creation

Personal freedom evolves and depends on a still mind. The key to creation is simple, yet can seem wickedly evasive. This is especially true if you're listening to those tapes playing in your head. The mind remains necessary, organizing your life and controlling your body. If you are in control of your mind, it will exist as your friend. If not you're going to have some very interesting experiences, to say the least. I remember a time when my mind seemed almost impossible to stop. Then I developed the BLISS exercise.

Let's create a scenario to illustrate how creation takes place. Just visualize a huge space ship. (I can't resist this.) The interior is lined with amethyst crystals and the ship is powered by inaudible sounds. The voyage is intergalactic. The mission is to chart the unknown possibilities of our existence. This mission is a vital one because the longevity and safety of the entire universe, your universe included, depends on it's success. The mission, should you decide to take it, is to allow your dreams to become a reality. The mission has a Captain, 1st officer, engineer and a crew. The Captain carries out the orders of the "Galactic Command Center". Being the gateway to other worlds, the "Galactic Command Center" has the ability to manifest anything. The "Galactic Command Center" connects to the universal spirit and the phenomenon of unconditional love called "God". It possesses unlimited awareness. The pulse beating at the core of the "G.C.C." feels like what we earthlings call "inner peace".

The "Galactic Command Center" will choose a Captain for this journey. Like any Captain, she will be responsible for the safety of the crew and ship. Making every decision on behalf of the expedition, she depends on the accuracy of the data received from the 1st officer, engineer and crew. Every action the Captain takes determines the ship's experiences. The Captain's name is your birth name. For example, the Captain of my ship is Theresa. The 1st officer, engineer and crew are other identities and you take on for your particular journey. By virtue of the fact you choose certain identities over others and place them in your consciousness, you entrust them to sit behind the controls of your ship called **"life"**.

What types of experiences will the ship and its crew encounter on this journey and how will they handle these experiences? Who would you like to see sitting behind those controls creating your experiences? Your Mother? How about your Father? Of course not, YOU want to be in control of your ship and your life. You want to run your personal universe. Yet unknowingly, many people allow identities from their mother and father to control their ship. You must not forget that **you** are the "Galactic Command Center." The "Galactic Command Center" is your higher-self and your higher-self is a spiritual energy that wants to discover and explore. It craves experiences. Since identities direct and mold your experiences, you as the Captain need to consciously elect a 1st officer, engineer and crew members who will align creatively with YOUR CHOICES. They must have the wisdom to not attract alien attacks. In order to help you accomplish your mission, your crew must know how to magnetically attract and hold the contents of your dreams. They must all be courageous explorers. Any member of the ship's crew even slightly slipping out of alignment, must be dismissed. The dismissal need not be permanent, because they can be sent to "sick bay" for testing and a transformational session of NeuroPhysical Reprogramming. Don't worry there are countless jobs available in other universes, right? So right now, set a course for your dreams. When selecting a crew to help you navigate carefully design each job description. My crew was selected on the basis of the following criterion. Each member had to be totally ethical, courageous, wise, and in 100% alignment with my mission. My instructions were and are to fearlessly and joyously explore the unknown, creating magical experiences. When you're truly in charge of your mission you will find yourself smack in the middle of experiencing joy.

To stay in control of your mission you must trust your intuition. There is no room for fear of the unknown on this journey. You can attribute any fear you have to an undissolved identity. But by moving forward in your evolution, you can take steps to dissolve this identity. As we discussed in Chapter 1, there is absolutely no point in over analyzing life, unless you want to become an analytical zombie forever stuck in the past. This "analytical" identity's function is to constantly "figure out". But as long as you stay in your head trying to "figure things out" you won't experience life or feelings.

There is power in logic and a flaw. Power coming from how forcefully logic convinces you of its infallible correctness when making any decision on it's basis alone. The flaw? For logic alone to prevail it must ignore and suppress the existence of intuition. When logic and intuition are allowed to co-exist they each benefit from the other, but if logic alone rules, your inherent wisdom can be buried under your fear of the unknown.

Recover Your Natural State Of Grace

Although, you may learn about yourself through hypnotherapy or some other modality tapping into your unconscious mind, the laser-like tool I call NeuroPhysical Reprogramming™ offers you the best chance of deciphering the language of the unconscious. Through discovering the foundation programming of the unconscious, you will discover specific identities you may wish to release. N.P.R. actually decodes the energy patterns in Meta-Consciousness and assists you in the speedy recovery of your natural state of grace. What does it feel like to be in a natural state of grace? It's a steady peaceful rhythm exuding and expanding from yourself.

Society seems to be on an endless quest searching for the answer to the question, "What is the meaning of life?". Life's meaning lies deep within each of us and can be accessed through self-empowerment. As a self-empowered person you know your value, you know your purpose here on earth, and you feel a passion that drives you forward. It's possible the meaning of life is simply to experience passion, joy and love. My point, *you* create the true meaning of *your* life not someone outside yourself.

How do behavioral patterns, identities and beliefs get stored in Meta-Consciousness? We have all heard stories of how one child in a family can become a priest and another a convicted felon. How can this be? The answer lies not only in your belief systems and your environment but how your belief system reflects your world view. In addition, there may be a karmic factor involved. If you believe in the theory of cause and effect, (The theory being for every action there is a reaction), that's called karma. *The New*

Lexicon Webster's Dictionary gives the following definition, "the power, resulting from an individuals volitional acts, which determines his cycle of reincarnations, before he attains release from this world; (Buddhism and Hinduism) the sum total of the acts done in one stage of a person's existence, which determine his destiny in the next stage; (Jainism) a form of matter which can contaminate a soul and postpone it's attaining Nirvana". Obviously, you don't have to be Buddhist or Hindu in order to understand and accept the karmic principles of life. Other religions have similar theoretical doctrines. In fact, I don't see accepting karmic principles as necessarily meaning you have chosen them to the exclusion of other religions or forms of worship. Karma is a state of awareness and consciousness. This is why the theory of karma is accepted in physics because every chemical action has a reaction.

Here's another example of the invisible nature in the formation of identifies and beliefs. Let's take a look at a family of six: two parents with four children. One child looks up to mom and takes on her beliefs. The next child thinks that Dad really has it wired, and takes on his beliefs. The third thinks Mom and Dad are O.K., but the next door neighbor is the one she really thinks is cool, so she takes on the neighbor's beliefs. The fourth child loves Mom and Dad, likes the neighbor and finds his teacher *amazing*,. This child takes on the beliefs of his family, the neighbor and the teacher.

A child raised in a family experiencing financial struggle presents yet another scenario where genetics inform the evolution of an identity and the many resulting belief systems. This child feels his parents' fear, "there's never enough money". The child "identifies" with this belief and expands it to include "there is a lack of money in the world.". As the child becomes a teenager and later an adult, he experiences, with little variation, the same difficulty with money he saw when living with his parents. His unconscious resistance in the belief of a "lack of money" creates the reality of a "lack of money." in his life. This reinforces his fear. Additionally, this belief may be imprinted on his cellular DNA and remain completely invisible to him. He would be entirely unaware that he's creating this experience for himself. He might simply think, "that's just the way life is." and take this on as a belief. This identity's energy pattern would be stored in Meta-Consciousness and then reinforced through his childhood environment.

By tracing back to our resisted emotions and locating our hidden identities and beliefs we're able to make profound changes in our lives. When we let go of resistance, we make room for new and more beneficial identities and beliefs.

How do we know that our genetic blueprint contains behavioral patterns and programs? Perhaps thousands of case histories are known of adopted children who have never met their biological parents until late in life, well past the formative years. These children were never exposed to their biological parents' belief systems or emotions. Yet, when as adults they meet their biological parents, they notice incredible similarities in their behavioral patterns and manner of emotionality and lifestyle choices. The only way to accurately account for this phenomena is by accepting the premise that identities, behavioral patterns and emotionality all originate from a genetic blueprint.

How Can I Create Inner Peace?

I know you desire access to the sacred part of your soul which is always tranquil. But how do we access this place? Meditation can guide us there. How long do we need to mediate? An hour? More? The answer is no, not any more. Through the use of simple tools you can handle stress on a daily basis. These tools, "The Reality Shifting Exercises" at the back of the book, assist you in experiencing a profound level of tranquillity. When used daily these tools not only assist you in attaining the sacred place of tranquillity, but they have a cumulative effect and soon you'll be able to reach your place of tranquillity almost instantaneously, whenever you desire. It has never been more clear. The reality you create depends on you and the nature of your conscious and unconscious choices.

"Hope" Is A Natural State

"Hope" is an inborn state of being we all have access to, some call it "faith". These are both merely labels we use to describe a feeling. These feelings are uplifting. Do not despair if you had no model for "hope" in your childhood, you can still access this state.

Because of the importance computers will play in the future, our educational system stresses the need for today's students becoming computer literate. Yet somehow this same educational system overlooks one of the most essential aspects of our individual futures, the ability to create success and happiness for ourselves. Our schools totally ignore teaching children to explore their feelings and belief systems, both of which will have a huge impact on the quality of their futures. Our childhood schooling stresses intelligence over wisdom or intuition. Children in America do not learn about their bodies. Children in America do not have classroom education involving how best to handle their anger, their fear or their feelings of low self esteem. Children in America are not learning how to use their innate power and strength to create a better world. Why? Is there a plot to keep us ignorant and dependent on the medical establishment? It's an interesting question, isn't it?

As children we learn many ways of giving our power away from watching the adults in our life give away their power. We're taught to be ignorant about our bodies and raised to consult all manner of experts who we entrust with decision-making power over our health. Due to low self-esteem acquired in childhood, we continually try to make others feel they're wrong, so we can feel we're right. This identity is responsible for wars. Children are taught at an early age about fighting wars to survive.

We must look to ignite the flame of hope by educating our children to all the possibilities. When people are bereft of hope, changes take place in their biochemistry, in the processes and cells of the brain and in their regenerative powers. Several years ago Joseph Chilton Pierce in "Evolution's End", described the prospect of a "hole in brain development", when a child does not experience a significant enough amount of storytelling during critical stages of the child's brain maturation. He postulated this leads to deficits in the individual's scope of imagination and aptitude for abstract thinking, in particular mathematical reasoning. Young teens begin to experience emotional difficulty when they feel pain, and are unable to imagine the pain ever ending. They are living without the prospect of hope, which is the ability to imagine there being different outcomes from those we're facing. This creates a void in the person's consciousness. There's a temptation to fill this void with mind changing drugs. Is today's rampant drug culture the result of a lack of imaginary skills and experiences? The kind of skills children gain when they are told storytales. Starting with children, our society trains us to take pills to stop ourselves from feeling anything. It is a learned response. The only way to correct the inhumane treatment of our children, is to replace the pills with unconditional love and education. The education should include how to handle our bodies, our minds, our emotions and use unconditional love as a parenting tool in society. Whether prescription drugs, over-the-counter or off the street, a pill can not fill the void. For someone who's never experienced "hope" the word is meaningless. Would you want your child and every child to know the true meaning of the word "hope"? Did you want to know when you were a child? It's not too late, "hope" is a natural and recurring feeling. Ever since your existence as a spiritual being it's been in your innate cellular intelligence.

Mass consciousness is a powerful thing. We are constantly bombarded, through the media with negativity and this breeds a sense of hopelessness. We start taking it personally and believe the negativity to be happening to us as a part of our daily life. We become part of the mass mind set and allow others to do our thinking and feeling. We get hard pressed to focus inward and recognize our feelings and our own deeper consciousness. The solution is not found through someone or something outside of ourselves. The solutions to the problems on this planet are buried deep within your own consciousness. You must embrace and deeply explore your inner spiritual essence. It is uniquely yours and through it you can become your own authority. Enabling you to bring forth your contribution to the creation of an enlightened planetary civilization.

You don't need to worship a Guru in order to find enlightenment. Evolving to a high level of spiritual awareness of God is easy when you're sitting on the top of a mountain alone. But when you're working and driving the freeways in L.A., creating a high spiritual awareness is quite a different matter. Close relationships will stretch your awareness of self and strengthen your connection to the cosmos. The best Guru to learn from is the one living inside of you.

So Your Empowered - Now What?

Now, create your dream. You know, the wish you've always wanted to become true. The emotional support necessary to create this dream may have been missing in the past. You buried your desire, pretending none of it mattered. Perhaps you judged it a silly childhood fantasy, not an intelligent "adult" decision.

Imagine becoming self-empowered. Now, feel self-empowered. Imagine a life where your dreams come true. Feel what it's like to have dreams come true. Your dream isn't silly, it will bring you joy. Dreams are never stupid when they expand your ability to feel love. They are what they are and your dream can become a reality. How, do you start this manifestation? Just follow the formula below and you're on your way.

The Formula For Creating Your Dreams!

1. Get focused on your dreams and goals. Write down and complete the action steps necessary to manifest your dreams.

2. Be aligned with your goals. If you doubt your ability to create your dreams, they won't manifest.

3. Tell the truth, do not hold in your feelings, express them. Find a way to live your truth!

4. Love unconditionally!

5. Embrace your dragons. Do not fight with them. When you fight dragons they appear to grow stronger.

6. Enjoy the journey!

"Fear Of The Unknown

Is An Illusion That Is Created

To Keep One From Boredom!"

Chapter 3
The Brain and Transformation
(made easy)

O.K., it's time you were acquainted with your brain. Let's explore how identities affect your brain chemistry, and in turn your personal experience.

The brain functions like an antenna, receiving and transmitting frequencies. The brain and the spinal cord comprise the central nervous system. They are enclosed and protected within the bony structures of the skull and spinal column.

The spinal cord is like an antenna, **receiving** information conveyed from the nerves of the skin, joints, muscles and ligaments, and for movement **sends** motor commands.

The Limbic System

The Limbic System, labeled the emotional or primitive old brain, is a network of nerve centers above the hypothalamus. This is where Meta-Consciousness™ is located. Research with NeuroPhysical Reprogramming indicates when you experience memories of the past, either as a past life or an alternate reality. This comes from the old or primitive brain. The Limbic System is connected to both the cortical centers in the temporal lobes (related to thought and higher cognitive functions) and the hypothalamus. It is additionally involved in anger, fright, aggression, hunger and sexual arousal. This dual relationship permits emotions to reach conscious awareness, allowing for cognitive fantasies and observations that affect us emotionally. The hypothalamus functions as an integral part of the processing of our thoughts. When a thought surfaces, the thought goes through the hypothalamus for processing. In order to change a behavior you must eliminate the thoughts, identities and belief systems creating the behavioral *pattern.* One must catch the thought at its onset and eliminate it along with the belief and identity *before* it processed through the hypothalamus. The entire energy pattern must be dissolved. Then and only then will a permanent reality shift and behavior change occur. What is the secret to changing your life? First, you have to be aligned with the desire to change. The next step, is to be aware of negative thoughts and the moment you notice the presence of a negative thought, embrace the feeling by becoming the thought. Breathe deeply and keep feeling, soon the thought should dissipate. As you breathe, the oxygen will carry the thought's energy pattern to the surface allowing you to feel even deeper. By becoming the energy pattern and immersing yourself in it, you are actually melting away any fear and resistance. I use my Neuro-Emotional Remedies or the instrumentals on the "5 Element Healing" and "Synchrony" compact discs to dissolve the energy pattern as soon as it is fully experienced. If you cannot catch a thought at its onset, do not worry, make a note of the experience and deliberately resurface the thought at a later time. Then feel it until it dissolves.

The amygdala, part of the limbic system, contains the highest concentration of opiate receptors in the brain. Opiate receptors relieve chronic pain and can be stimulated by releasing identities.

Temporal Lobe

Where do those déjà vu experiences originate? The temporal lobe of the brain. The temporal lobe controls hearing, memory and the sense of self and time. This indicates déjà vu experiences come from a memory, somewhere in time.

Occipital Lobe

The occipital lobe is the visual center of the brain, controlling and transforming the data received and conveyed from the retina of the eye. It is my personal belief that the temporal and occipital lobes are responsible for the kind of experiences we call "spacing out". I'm using the term "spacing out" to describe the phenomena which takes place when you're driving and arrive safely at your destination but can't remember the trip or how you got there.

What! We Have Interference Patterns In Our Brain?

It has been documented through experiments on human subjects that unconscious, or fleeting thoughts and beliefs actually register in the brain. A filtering process was noted by Freud, which he called repression. The brain selectively transmits through a filtering process, first to the unconscious mind, then to the conscious mind. My research indicates this filtering process is an energy pattern containing one or more identities, which sets up an interference pattern repressing an experience or emotion.

The brain electro-magnetically sends and receives information, like a radio station. Identities filter out certain experiences creating your perception. Have you ever noticed how one individual will perceive a movie, a communication, or an action one way, while another individual will perceive the same thing, but very differently. Your beliefs and identities actually create your perception. Identities filter out experiences like sun glasses filter out suns rays.

The brain also sends, transmitting chemical and electromagnetic signals. The messages you receive and how you perceive these messages depends on the identities through which you see life. What we perceive also depends on the level of consciousness we're attuned to in life. The verbal and non-verbal messages you send to another person will be received and understood by them according to the identities they possess and assert. However, you could be sending both conscious and unconscious communication, in other words conflicting messages. This would account for a person receiving "mixed signals" and feeling confused. This unconscious communication could be a hidden agenda. A hidden agenda is a concealed communication, perhaps a desire or a feeling. Hidden agendas are always problematic, creating dissonance instead of resonance, even if you believe the agenda is another benefit.

You can now easily see how the brain is a complex sending and receiving station for cellular communication and communication to others. When a person creates a physical illness there is some pre-existing decision and an identity in some part of the brain interfering with the normal communication to the organ or gland. When we want to manifest a new reality, any doubts we have concerning our ability to create this new reality will act as a type of interference, a filter, keeping the new, more desirable reality from manifesting. The communication or frequency needed to manifest the new reality never gets through to the brain or to the body. The communication is blocked. We are foiled by the identity's doubts.

Neurotransmitters

The brain produces neurotransmitters such as norepinephrine, epinephrine, dopa, dopamine, serotonin and acetylcholine.. These neurotransmitters are important for emotional stability, sleep, memory, learning, perception, vision and muscle movement. There are non-toxic substances such as amino acids which stimulate neurotransmitter production. This may prove to be very helpful in the safe treatment of many neurological disorders. Furthermore, I feel it is wiser to take an amino acid for a condition relating to deficient or excessive neurotransmitter production, rather than take a drug which produces side effects. A memory related condition such as Alzheimer's disease would be one such example of a condition which might be helped by the administering of amino acids.

References

Harry Oldfield and Roger Coghill. *The Dark Side of the Brain*
Richard Restak, MD. *The Mind*

Chapter 4
Belief Systems, Your Body and Aging

Have you ever heard someone say, "I'm sick and tired...?" Well, they probably are! People usually make such statements when they're under stress or emotionally aggravated. Heightened emotional states, especially those we don't wish to feel, create a perfect breeding ground for illness. Through my research and private practice, I've noticed the increasing relationship between an individual's resistance to expressing feelings and emotions, and the occurrence of accelerated aging.

Chronic Fatigue Equals Chronic Resistance

One ugly truth certain to haunt you if you continue to resist an experience is: *Whatever you resist will persist!* Chronic Fatigue is a label describing a condition where the immune system, by being suppressed brings about the symptoms of sever fatigue, allergies to foods and environmental pollutants. Candida, a fungal yeast, is often present with Chronic Fatigue. These two conditions respond very well to N.P.R. I have had many patients heal both conditions within one month of treatment. Any condition which affects the immune system can be eliminated by eliminating judgments, removing the labels and taking the resistance off of various emotional fears about life. Many people are so paranoid they fear eating. This equates to resistance.

Although there are many myths and mass consciousness beliefs about foods, like sugar, red meat or fat being deadly, your repressed emotions are more deadly than the aforementioned foods. It's true these food are unhealthy. After all, anything is unhealthy in large enough quantities. You don't have to buy into the fear and anxiety which has been created around food. You can make a choice and that feels comfortable without feeling guilty. You can eat a healthful diet without neurosis or paranoia. I have personally tried every diet known to man (and woman). As a result of the resistance and judgment I had on food, I created a metabolic dysfunction. Due to the severity of my extremely strict diet(s), I started judging others' nutritional habits.

Now, I am not saying if you have a physical or emotional illness you should go hog wild and eat anything you want. A person with an illness will greatly benefit their health by following a strict diet to strengthen their immune system and remove the burden of foods which are hard to digest when laden with toxic chemical substances and parasites. There is one factor that has proved to be extremely beneficial to my patients. This is the elimination of all drugs. I consider drugs, including aspirin, to be more toxic than red meat, sugar or fat. Any toxic substance accelerates the aging process due to the fact it is a toxin.

How do you know which diet is good for your body when there are so many belief systems about food and body types? I personally don't see the value in labeling yourself with a particular "body type". Body types are used in Ayurvedic Medicine. They box you into, yet another belief system. I find the most objective way of determining the appropriate diet for an individual is to use kinesiological testing and common sense. I have used my own version of kinesiological testing (N.P.R.) with patients, testing supplements and diet for well over a decade. It not only works, it saves you the stress of being on a diet roller coaster. You can find out exactly what your body wants, right now. You can also learn how to test yourself using NeuroPhysical Reprogramming. Each test is accurate for approximately three to six months and then you need to re-test. Why re-test? Your body may have different requirements due to a change in a stress level you are currently experiencing. Furthermore, your body may want a change. Lets face it, some of us have hedonistic desires. To deny yourself something you crave for a long period of time may create stress. On the other hand, if you're aware that a food is extremely harmful to you, and you still eat it: you may have an identity trying to sabotage your progress or *your life*. For example, if you are a diabetic and you insist on eating sugar you are sabotaging your health.

The amount of effort Americans place on trying to look like a "super model" keeps our attention focused on finding physical faults with ourselves and everyone else. The most important thing is to create a physically fit, toned and trim body. Therefore, cardiovascular exercise is a must. Let's see those muscles! The human body was made for movement and even though snails move - that's not the kind of movement I had in mind.

Your creative intention and the choices you make give birth to your physical appearance and the physiological condition of your body. For example, if you believe your body is exactly like your father's, then your body will coax itself into forming according to the identity of your father. I radically changed the appearance of my body just by changing identities.

Chronological aging occurs every year, but biological aging reflects your perception of human aging. Aging does not have to accelerate to the point of degeneration, unless that is your expectation. Simply put, whatever you are programmed to believe, will be what you experience. A mass consciousness belief about biological aging states that it's "normal", that it "happens to everyone", but we know it doesn't happen to everyone at the same rate. Deep in your subconscious is a program about aging. By changing the program you can change your physical appearance and health. In other words, if you choose to take responsibility and spend more time on exploring your identities and beliefs, a change will come. It will happen and be worth it, but only if you think your worth it! Mass consciousness expects chronological aging to produce symptoms such as aches and pains when associated with labels like arthritis. Does your belief system include spending years in a nursing home, dependent on drugs or HMO's.? To me that is not even an option.

The human body naturally creates a continuous detoxification, regeneration, and cellular renewal. Therefore, it is possible to slow down our biologica! aging process as much as 10 to 20 years less than our chronological age. Now, for those who believe they are an unlimited being, why not stay feeling and looking as good as you did at 30 years old?

When you want to eliminate a belief about your body, about a disease, or aging, first find the identity creating the belief and feel it from *inside* yourself. Ask yourself: "What kind of person would hold this belief?" The answer will emerge. Then feel like the identity. When making a new goal concerning your body, you need to experience the goal as profoundly as you can. Breathe..., feel it all the way down to your toes and up to the top of your head.

Is Your Weight Like A YO-YO?

Controlling your weight can be handled in much the same way. Many people struggle with their weight. They resist their appearance and physical body. The resistance means you have your attention focused on your weight. By having your attention on this issue, the problem appears to grow bigger. In other words, your resistance feeds the problem. The answer to permanent weight loss and maintenance is to locate the precise identity, and it's *belief systems,* which causes the weight to manifest itself in the first place. Remember, an identity is merely a character playing out a role in your life. The identity could have nothing to do with the weight gain itself, it's roots could be related to some belief system based on fear from early childhood. Start with the Reality Shifting Exercises in this book. You may want to extend and continue to the next level, The Meta-Wellness Home Study Program. If you do not locate the cause of the weight gain, you will recreate the same pattern again. As you are now well aware, the problems with obesity are not limited to excessive eating or glandular problems. The direct relationship to any weight issue is how you feel - consciously and unconsciously - about yourself. You must empower yourself to locate and release the unconscious root cause, the *identity*, which is creating the problem and only then will the results be permanent.

Creating Vitality

The following list is an integral part of my lifestyle and one that I suggest patients follow.

1. Drink 8 to 10, 8 oz. glasses of water daily. Drink reverse osmosis water to avoid contamination with heavy metals, bacteria, flouride and parasites.
2. Amino acids and good quality protein (like deep sea fish) may be a necessary addition to your diet.

3. Exercise is essential for the body. It distributes nutrients through out the body and detoxifies the body from the effects of stress, including the effects of a stressful beliefs systems.
4. Touch, care and nurturing.
5. For an active body putting out a lot of energy, the inclusion of minerals and Vitamins A, B, C or E to the diet is essential. Creating and **resisting** stress in your life uses up several nutrients, like minerals, the B-vitamins and Vitamin C. Additionally, Vitamin C is great for your skin because it synthesizes collagen. Free Form Amino Acids are essential if you work out regularly.
6. A good digestion is essential. Eat fruits like papaya or take digestive enzymes.
7. Eat raw vegetables, vegetables are alive. The green vegetables capture more **awareness, light and chlorophyll.** Foods high in awareness and light assist our cells in the process of regeneration. Every meal should consist of at least 40% vegetables.
8. Eliminate saturated fats, like animal fats and fats from dairy products. Research has indicated saturated fats will eventually clog the arteries. Deep sea fish have natural oils which are excellent for the cardiovascular system.
9. Substitute natural sugars, like raw honey, for white sugar.
10. Eliminate chemicals like preservatives, MSG, or artificial colorings and flavorings.
11. Eliminate commercial anti-perspirants which contain aluminum chlorhydrate. Stop using aluminum cookware, try glass or stainless steel.

In addition to the above, if you would like to detoxify you body, lose weight, increase energy and stamina you may follow the additional suggestions below;

Eliminate milk products, red meat, poultry, alcohol, caffeine and fried foods. If you're afraid of feeling too good try this program for only 1 month. If you want to feel 10 years younger, embrace this program for 2 months. If you already eat a healthful diet and you're still feeling ill or possessing poor energy - the cause may be layers of identities.

Since Time And Space

Create Infinite Dimensions

And Occur Simultaneously,

There Is

No Limit To What We Can

Experience.

Chapter 5
Cellular Intelligence and Your Destiny

The time has come in our society to embrace new viewpoints about health and longevity. People no longer want to be kept in the dark about their overall health, they want to be empowered to self-heal. Observing the many books currently being published on the subject of consciousness and healing, it's easy to see the new attitude our society has taken. Books that were not accepted by the majority of the population two years ago are now going "main stream".

Your cellular intelligence is not a myth, but rather "the bottom line" in the creation of all realities. Many scientists have the opinion that it is difficult to make a cellular or genetic change, yet that's exactly what happens when any disease is permanently eliminated.

Physicists and Bio-physicists are going beyond the physical boundaries of emotional, mental and spiritual planes. They are delving into the physics of telepathy, intuition, universal consciousness and alternate realities. Their research led them to the profound revelation that every cell has an innate intelligence which controls the functioning of all systems within our bodies and our consciousness. My intuition tells me that this innate intelligence mirrors each individual's universe and forms our "reality".

The basis for this revelation began in 1923 when Dr. Alexander Gurwitsch discovered that light particles, or "photons", exist in all living things. Previously, photons were only known to exist in the earth, water and air. Therefore, Dr. Gurwitsch called the photons found in the cells of animals, plants and humans, "Bio-photons". All living things, without exception, emit Bio-photons. Bio-photons are not to be confused with phosphorescence or the bio-luminescence of the glow worm.

Dr. Gurwitsch realized that Bio-photons are light signals which guide our life processes and are stored in the cell's DNA.

DNA, Deoxyribonucleic Acid, is a giant molecule in the nucleus of every cell. It contains the total genetic heredity, or "blueprint" of the present living system. It would literally take ten thousand books to duplicate the information contained in one DNA molecule, located in one cell. It's important to note that stored within the cell's DNA is the entire hereditary holographic blueprint of your entire organism.

In 1975, about fifty years after Dr. Gurwitsch's discovery, Dr. Fritz A. Popp, of Marburg, Germany, found physical evidence to prove Gurwitsch's findings. In a dramatic demonstration at the Max Plank Institute for Astronomy in Heidelberg, Dr. Popp succeeded, through the use of a photo-multiplier, in making a single cell's Bio-photons visible on a TV screen. The photo-multiplier was so powerful, it could detect a firefly 10 km away. Dr. Popp found, "the existence of this radiation (the light in a cell) could no longer be denied."

A colleague tried to discredit Dr. Popp's work by saying Bio-photons are unimportant, because they're so weak. Dr. Popp replied, "One could insist that each thought is also insignificant because it cannot be traced physically, or because it lies below the physical objective detection range."

When Bio-photons were observed on a luminescent screen, they appeared to burst forth in thread-like flashes of light wrapped in a bundle.

Since it's possible to count the amount of light flickering and measure their emission, it's already been concluded that a stockpile of Bio-photons are stored in the DNA of every cell. The actual function of Bio-photons is to control the cell's growth. The Bio-photons create an intracellular balance which produces harmony. The harmony in turn creates cellular equilibrium within the cell and then all the parts function in synchronicity.

When the living organism experiences excessive stress on the mental, emotional or physical planes, the equilibrium of the cell is disturbed, and Bio-photon emissions are altered. For example, cancer cells radiate Bio-photons measurably stronger than healthy ones, because they are using up the cells' Bio-photon stores. When the depository of Bio-photons is exhausted, the cell dies. Disharmonic vibrations create disturbed energy patterns that dissipate the cell's ability to function efficiently. With its equilibrium askew, the cell cannot repair itself, and growth is inhibited. Unless the equilibrium is re-established, disease is inevitable.

The Bio-photon emissions are the DNA's way of communicating information to other cells. Thus, neither good nor bad information dies, it only gets transferred. Consequently, it's logical to conclude that when a cancerous cell is killed by chemotherapy, even as it's dying, it will transmit it's information to other cells. And in turn, they will receive and assimilate the cancerous cells' information into their DNA codes. This is why cancer can go into remission and resurface in the body at a later time.

Further observation indicates that every second 10 million cells die and are promptly replaced, meaning we actually have the ability to stay young if we eliminate the identity causing accelerated aging. This phenomenon cannot simply be a matter of bio-chemical reactions, if it were, it would take a much longer time. Instead, regeneration occurs at the speed of light. Unfortunately, disease can be transmitted just as quickly.

One truly important realization found, that until they are eliminated, identities will continue burdening a cell and the entire organism. So I focused my attention on creating a technology that released identities. I noticed that the disharmonic frequencies of an identity, though invisible to the naked eye, still have an energetic form. For example, by simply stepping into someone's physical space, you can "feel" their anger, chronic illness or depression.

Once an organ stores an identity's disharmonic energy pattern, it can take from five to fifteen years, and even longer before it manifests itself as a disease. My patients have often remarked, "I'm eating all the right things and I caught a cold. Everyone at work has one." The truth is, you cannot "catch" anything unless you believe you can. Disease is a physical manifestation stemming from a repressed emotion attatched to an identity and a belief that attracts a cold. Even after being in close contact with critically ill and so-called "contagious" patients, I never contracted an illness from them. So the key is to stay neutral and fearless.

The good news is, there are beneficial identities, ones that serve us. Once the disharmonic or unhealthy identity is experienced and eliminated, it can be replaced by a more beneficial one resulting in the DNA regaining it's equilibrium. Once balanced, cellular repair begins and the immune system is strengthened. If disease is present, the strengthened immune system produces the appropriate anti-bodies, and healing takes place. The proper vitamins and minerals from fresh fruits, vegetables and grains are also essential for cellular repair.

Often times an identity can contain disharmonic as well as harmonic frequencies. For example, when a child or young female is told she's, "just like her mother", she will "identify" with all aspects of being her mother. At her age, she may have trouble filtering out the wanted traits from the unwanted ones. Therefore, if that wonderful mother happens to later contract breast cancer, the child could very possibly manifest the same disease later in life.

Extreme resistance or desire acts as a warning that some belief and identity needs to be explored and released. Like a magnet, you attract whatever you resist and push away whatever you "extremely" desire. Any extreme may be an obsession. Try to identify and feel both states, breathing deeply. There are several exercises in my courses that adequately handle extreme resistance and desire.

By breathing deeply while exploring the identity, oxygen lifts the energy pattern to the conscious level where it can be experienced and released. Your perception transforms "the event" from an emotionally charged trauma, to a memory in the tapestry of your life. Once dissolved, the energy pattern will never be replicated.

Presently, there are two major models for treating disease; the first is the bio-chemical theory and the second is the holistic approach. Bio-chemists view the human body as a chemical chain reaction, triggered by enzymes. They believe physical conditions are simply deviations of bio-chemical reactions within the organism. Yet, Bio-chemists have never been able to explain why enzymes choose to initiate chemical reactions at one time and not initiate them at another time. They have yet to acknowledge the research proving that electro-magnetic radiation and electro-magnetic couplings activate enzymes. Consequently, when they view abnormal energy patterns of Bio-photons in the ultra-violet range, they interpret them as insufficient chemical reactions, diagnosing and treating the patient for a metabolic disturbance. A more accurate interpretation could be that there is either an overabundant or insufficient Bio-photon emission or stockpile in the DNA.

The holistic point of view holds that humans are influenced by their environmental conditions. Meditation, body work, supplements and diet can all help support a positive change bringing new awareness and successful results. The problem with this approach is, it too can create a dependency on authority figures, gurus, masters, vitamin pills and diets.

The model which seems to be the most effective for healing is one in which we are no longer a victim of our environment. By eliminating identities which attract physical weakness or are too easily affected by the environment, the body will naturally return to it's proper balance.

My training in Germany included the therapeutic use of "Ultra Fine" frequency technology, which basically consisted of a filter and an amplifier. The more I observed, the more I became convinced that all energy patterns, even identities and thoughts, can be inverted (reversed), being amplified or eliminated.

Very simply, most of our feelings originate from our thoughts. Unless we have learned a technique to keep ourselves "out of our head", we're probably in some way a slave to our feelings. When we are detached and without an emotional stake in an outcome, we are able to *choose* how to respond to people and events... even our own thoughts. In this state we can let disharmonic frequencies or negativity pass through us as if we were invisible or we can choose to reinforce and amplify them. We truly have freedom of choice and are no longer at the mercy of outside conditions.

In summary, wellness is a constantly flowing state of grace, the lack of resistance to experience and feeling. Wellness is always there, waiting for you to discover it and embrace it.

REFERENCES

1. Dr. Wolfgang Ludwig. *Ontology* , a paper
2. Harry Oldfield and Roger Coghill. *The Dark Side of the Brain*
3. Dr. Fitz Popp. *Electromagnetic Bio-Information*
4. Richard Restak, MD. *The Mind*

Chapter 5
Cellular Intelligence and Your Destiny
Definitions

Holography:
An image produced by wave-front reconstruction, specifically by using lasers to record on a photographic plate the diffraction pattern from which a 3-dimensional image can be projected.

Coupling:
To link circuits or currents by magnetic induction; to unite chemically; to link together.

Disequilibrium:
Lack of stability or equilibrium.

Oscillate:
1. To swing back and forth with a steady, uninterrupted rhythm.
2. To waver between more than one thought or course of action; to vacillate.
3. Physics. To vary between alternate extremes, usually within a definable time period.

Disharmonic:
Disharmony, unaligned.

Harmonic:
Healthy, in balance, aligned.

Morphogenetic:
A previously created form, having the ability to keep reproducing itself.

Chapter 6
The Rhythm Of The Universe

Sound is the most vital force in the universe. Like the way a heart beats, the rhythm of the universe is a constant movement of expansion and contraction. The sound of a heartbeat radiates throughout every cell of the human body, the beats creating a rhythm within the body. A rhythm, like a heart beat and a pulse, is made up of oscillations which can be measured on Western medical instruments and through Chinese pulse diagnosis. These rhythms produce electromagnetic waves, frequencies stored in the body's fluids and in every cell's memory.

Here on Earth there are sounds in nature, sounds are also produced in outer space. It's a well known fact that Dolphins, along with Whales and other life forms, communicate via frequencies.

Since we absorb sound effortlessly through our largest organ the skin, music therapy has the potential to act as a healing tool. Sound also absorbs through bone and is used in hospitals today to break-up and dissolve kidney stones. Traditional medicine uses "Ultra Sound" as a diagnostic and treatment modality.

As the correct musical frequencies come in contact with the skin, the acupuncture meridians are treated. In addition to the skin translating this information to the meridians, the ears send signals to the nervous system in a similar manner causing a change in neurotransmitter emissions. Don't forget the ear also has acupuncture points affected by sound frequencies.

It may be interesting to note that not all sounds are healthy. You know how listening to some music can give you a headache, or how scratching your nails on a blackboard sends chills up your spine Even thinking about it now can send chills up your spine. Music we like may not always have a positive effect on our cells. A perfect example of this is the use of sound for crowd control instead of tear gas. You can see how sound can be very powerful. Every sound and musical note produces a numerical frequency called hertz, (Hz). (See Chapter 1.)

For the purposes of healing, frequencies produced in acoustically performed music provide the human body with the type of frequencies needed to correct physical, mental and emotional imbalances.

Music And Medicine

Sound has been used for healing for centuries in many countries, for example England, Germany, India, and Sweden. In fact, music and medicine have been associated together since the beginning of recorded history. One of the earliest Egyptian documents on music is, in truth a prescription for music therapy. The healing powers of music were recognized by the Chinese, Hindus, ancient Greeks, Arabs, along with primitive cultures. Numerous references to these powers are found in both musical and medical writing of the 16th and 17th centuries. We are now reawakening the use of sound for purposes of healing ourselves.

During my research in Germany in magnetic field, sound, and color therapies I became fascinated with how the inner rhythms of the body are mirrored by the cosmic, universal rhythms. For example, the earth turns 1 degree every 4 minutes. The same as our heartbeat to breath ratio, 4 pulse beats per breath.

A logarithmic recording of the various body rhythms; muscle, skin, liver, circulation, blood pressure, respiration and pulse bears a remarkable resemblance to the cell's DNA double helix pattern. In physical terms, each frequency possesses a color and sound simultaneously. Each organ and gland responds to frequencies of sound, color, and homeopathic remedies.

Seeking a deeper meaning to our connection to the entire universe, I had the realization that everything in the universe is energetically related to everything else. Then I discovered additional correlations. For example, the rotation of the earth every 24 hours corresponds to the numerical hertz frequency of the musical note G and its octaves. This in turn corresponds to the cell's DNA resonance at a wavelength of 351/702 Nanometers. (One Nanometer is one billionth of a meter.)

Furthermore, European research has indicated that a range of octaves from different notes have a variety of emotional and physiological effects. According to the German research papers and books by award winning physicists, the note G and it's octaves promote physical growth, enhance the memory, and produce emotional enthusiasm for life. This could come from the note G's ability to once again balance the cellular DNA/RNA.

Advanced research by German Medical Doctor and Internist, Dr. Bodo Koehler has shown that musical notes have a correlation to color and to specific gemstones. For example, the color red correlates to the frequency of the musical note C. The color purple correlates to the frequency of 432 Hz and the musical note A. In Europe tests were conducted on unhealthy cells using sound frequencies. The unhealthy cells were exposed to many frequencies but the frequency that produced the most positive healing effect on the cell was 432 Hz and 435 1/2 Hz according to Dr. Wolfgang Ludwig, Diplomat Physicist. Testing indicated this frequency eliminated certain viruses from the cell, bringing the cell back to harmony.

How Can We Start Using Sound Therapy?

Very expensive high-tech instruments that heal with frequencies are used today to promote cellular healing. These instruments are not sold in the US and are produced by German manufacturers. These high-tech instruments are designed to dissolve energy patterns by producing color, sound, and magnetic fields. These are then emitted either from a soft laser beam, brass hand held electrodes or magnetic inductors. Then they're applied to acupuncture meridians or directly at an organ. There is a problem with this type of therapy. Unless you dissolve the entire energy pattern and locate the causal identity, the symptoms may move to another organ or return to the same organ. However, it is entirely possible to dissolve the entire energy pattern with some magnetic field therapy equipment. This equipment is priced at $10,000 to $40,000 US dollars. Some medical sound therapy systems, recorded on audio cassette tapes, are being sold worldwide to health practitioners for $150.00 or more per tape and just for one organ! Most of the tapes I have experimented with were synthetically produced by electronic instruments and were not very effective.

Well, you really don't have to own very expensive high-tech equipment. You can purchase books and tapes on "toning" with your voice and "sound healing", with acoustic instruments. I have been impressed by the positive effect of some Buddhist chants that awaken the senses. You might want to play with tuning forks which are tuned to specific frequencies. Crystal bowls have a beautiful resonance with harmonic overtones. I also like brass bowls for producing healing sounds. If you own an acoustic instrument try tuning it to 432 Hz, then experiment with feeling the effect of different notes in your body.

You can test the results of sound on each acupuncture meridian using electro-diagnosis. Unfortunately this is illegal in the US, unless you're a medical doctor and still you may have the local authorities breathing down your neck.

For well over a decade I was determined to make the sound frequency technology available and affordable to the general public. Originally I had the idea to create a cassette recording, but the delivery of the frequencies were not stable enough. If the cassette tape player is dirty or not working perfectly for some other reason, the frequency can be altered. As a matter of fact a cassette tape can stretch after only one or two plays making the frequencies unstable. Therefore, I decided to create the healing music on Compact Discs. This can also be problematic, because generally speaking compact discs do not reproduce all of the harmonics present in an acoustically produced instrumental. You can imagine my astonishment and relief when my testing indicated the two compact discs were recorded effectively and completely. There are two reasons why my recordings were successful. First, the specific notes (frequencies) were composed and performed in a repeated pattern related to each of the Five Elements. In addition, I modified the tuning to a specific frequency lower than the normal 440 Hz. So, tuning it down to 432 Hz is an extremely important step in the successful recording of these music therapy compact discs.

"5 Element Healing" and "Synchrony" were developed after a decade of my personal research. I combined the "Five Element Theory of Acupuncture" and "Fung Shui" as the basis for these healing albums. All of the instrumentals are composed and performed by Greg Wells, a recording artist who brings my research to life. "5 Element Healing" has five instrumentals and each one is composed of only 4 to 6 main notes. Each instrumental corresponds to an element and it's related organ, gland, meridian and emotion.

An acoustic grand piano, perfectly tuned to A-440 Hz- was used for the recording. Using an acoustic instrument is essential for healing vibrations. The healing vibrations occur because of the harmonic overtones. The harmonics carry the information, the healing frequency, into the body and thus the cell. The intended healing can be vibrated through the instrument by a person's hands making the harmonic overtones even more powerful. "Synchrony", my new album, combines the Air Element and Fung Shui. It was researched and produced with the same guidelines to achieve different levels of emotional clearing. One of the instrumentals entitled "Balance", assists you in recreating the passion and courage in your life. The sixth instrumental, "Mountain" has a profound effect on the releasing of foundation beliefs from Meta-Consciousness and assists in absorbing new desired identities when used with the N.P.R. protocol.

When you listen to music, choose a place without any distractions like outside noise or other music playing. To test the effect of any sound on your own body it's best to breathe deeply and expand your consciousness to contain and feel the sound. Listen and feel the effects of the frequencies. See if you can track the notes in different parts of your body. Children of all ages love playing with musical notes because it allows them the freedom to experience new realities.

My Secret Dream

I became interested in music as a very young child. My sister played the piano and I took lessons for a while. I felt insecure about my abilities because of the expectations and comparisons I felt from my family. My childhood experiences made me want to completely withdraw from the present reality. I found that music was the only thing which would shift my present reality so I could feel joy. I felt music in my heart and every cell of my body. I pretty much stayed out of the painful present and remained in one alternate reality after another. Sleeping was another escape, because I could dream in peace. Every night I had a reoccurring dream. I truly believe this dream saved my life. The dream helped me choose life. This dream was in my unconscious and acted as a reminder for me that there was something to look towards in the future. The dream never went away, not during my teenage years or during my adult life. Instead of the dream fading away, it grew stronger.

The dream took place on a stage in a theater or a music hall. I was singing and being accompanied by a pianist on a grand piano. We were healing the audience with unconditional love and sound. But this could only be a dream, I thought! I resisted manifesting my dream, because I had no experience in one major aspect of the dream. Singing! I imagined finding a musician who would send transformational vibrations to the audience through his hands. In the dream, as it starts to unfold, the performer's face was not visible. Approximately two years ago, I met a gifted musician who immediately understood the purpose of my project and agreed to compose and perform my research. After the second album, "Synchrony", was completed I realized just a part of the dream was fulfilled, the next step was to create guided concerts and workshops to assist planetary healing. "But what about my voice", I wondered. What if it sucks! I had not yet dared to share this aspect of my dream with another living soul. I was very insecure about my voice, with negative judgments clouding my reality. There was only one course of action to take - eliminate the identity that felt that way and create a new one, one that would serve me. In the dream, my voice resonated healing and love. It was beautiful. I knew somewhere deep inside of me that voice existed. All I had to do was nail down a great vocal technique which would allow me to transmit love through the sound of my voice.

I tried a few vocal gurus before I manifested a great vocal coach who was all I could have hoped for in the beginning. I was overjoyed when I discovered I actually liked my voice. So, my childhood dream has become my reality and everyone benefits. I have manifested the guided workshops/ concerts.

There's more. Sound and unconditional love are modalities that I will explore for the rest of my existence, learning to play life, like one would play an instrument.

"Schumann Waves"

The rhythm of the earth is controlled by many elements. You will be exploring information with regard to staying in harmony with our earth.   It is a fascinating area to explore, because our physiological and emotional health can be altered by not having enough *Schumann Waves.*

W.O. Schumann, a German scientist, discovered atmospheric resonances which were subsequently named Schumann fields.   Schumann waves are present between the earth's surface and the ionosphere, up to an altitude of around 100 km. They envelope the planet with rhythmic oscillations at a frequency of 7.8 Hz.   This 7.8 Hz frequency is critical by virtue of it's "hippocampal" (pituitary) frequency and is essential for normal body rhythms in all mammals. The importance here, is that the 7.8 Hz frequency aligns and connects us to the earth and the cosmos.   The formation of Schumann waves is related to the presence of adequate ground electro-conductivity and is maintained when the ground water level remains normal. Today the ground water level is no longer maintains the necessary ground conductivity. It has been lowered by the straightening of rivers, the utilization of ground water for industrial purposes and by insulating asphalt and sewer construction in the cities. Steel and concrete building also interfere with the Schumann waves. According to NASA's research, travel beyond the ionosphere, where Schumann waves are missing, leads to physiological disturbances such as nausea and fatigue. Theses can be corrected in flight by means of Schumann field generators. After Schumann generators were installed in space capsules these negative feelings ceased.

We Are A Mirror Of Our Universe!

To maintain a harmonious connection, so we're able to experience movement and a continuous flow in life, we must keep changing and growing, mirroring the universe and the planet earth. What would happen if the earth just stopped turning? We would not survive. When your life lacks movement, you feel "stuck" and depressed, giving the perception of illness. What's actually occurring is your evolution and movement has stopped because some layer of energy, an "identity", has disrupted the natural reflection of universal harmony. When this occurs, we experience symptoms like hormonal changes, aches, pains, organ or glandular dysfunctions and allergies.

My prescription for keeping life flowing is to live life in the gap, in other words, to stay in the present. There is an old saying I picked up along the way, "If you're not living on the edge, you're taking up too much space". There are other choices! You can live in the past, which produces depression or choose to live in the future, which causes paranoia or perhaps you'll alternate between three choices; past, present and future - which only creates confusion. Now that you know the choices - you simply need to make one. Then use the tools in this book to help you stay in the present.

Music Therapy Research

Kirlian Photography is known widely throughout the world as a diagnostic energetic testing modality in the field of complimentary medicine. But even though some countries, like England and Germany rely on Kirlian Photography, it's relatively unknown in the US. There are various types of Kirlian Photographic equipment available in the global marketplace. The technology going into the manufacturing of the equipment is quite extensive, so I will leave out all the technical stuff. First, photographic prints are taken of the hands and/

or the feet. In the research below, we used just the hands. A patient places his finger tips on a plate and then the photo is taken from beneath the plate. The purpose in using Kirlian Photography is to detect energy leaks or energy deficits in acupuncture meridians. Acupuncture meridians are energy channels that end on the hands and feet and on either side of the finger nail. (See diagram below.)

This means when the finger tips of the hands are photographed, the developed print will indicate spaces or gaps in the area next to a meridian. The gap means that the person does not have a full complement of energy in an acupuncture meridian. The two photographs below are of an AIDS patient, age 39. The top photograph was taken before an N.P.R. session. The "5 Element Healing" compact disc was used at the end of the session as an integral part of the elimination of his beliefs systems and identities. Each finger has one meridian on either side of the nail. You can see the energy leaks or the gaps around his finger tips. Let's take a look at his left hand. The finger tips of his left hand are on the left side of the page and the fingers of his right hand below and to the right. I have marked where the thumb is located so you can get an idea of the finger placement of the whole hand. The gaps on his 5th finger, the little finger (extreme left), indicates the Heart Meridian has an energy deficit (see the gap). The 4th finger has an energy deficit in his Endocrine Meridian (also known as the Triple Warmer Meridian). Now, lets go to the thumb where you can see an energy deficit in the Lung Meridian and the Lymph Meridian.

The second set of photographs are after the N.P.R. session. Notice that the gaps present in the first photograph are filled in on the second photograph.

Kirlian Photographs Of AIDS Patient

Before N.P.R. session.

Patient's left hand.

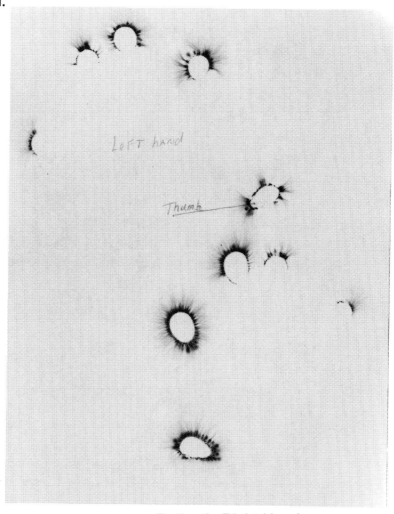

Patient's Right Hand

After N.P.R. Session and the integration of a new identity using "5 Element Healing".

Patient's left hand.

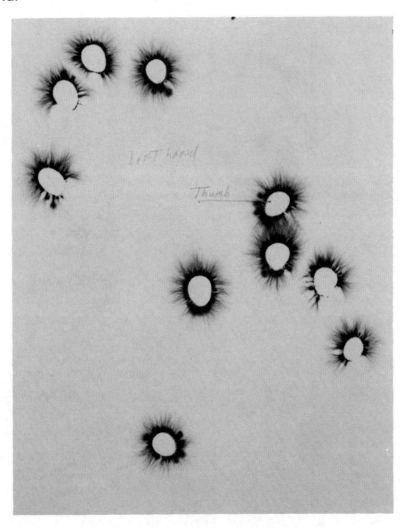

Patient's Right Hand

Below is the Kirlian Photography of my hands before and after giving the N.P.R. session to the above AIDS patient. Please note that I did not physically touch the patient during the session. I used a rubber glove on my left hand and did not touch him with my right hand. The "5 Element Healing" compact disc was played in the room near the patient.

#1 - My left hand before N.P.R. session.

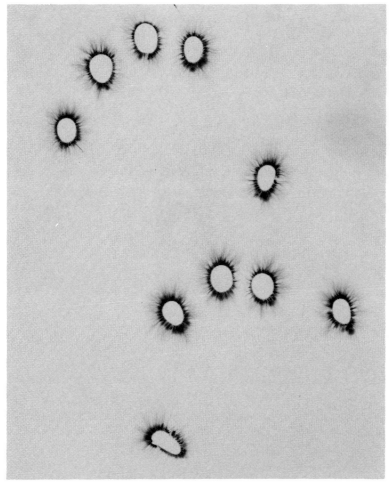

My Right Hand

#2 -My Left hand after N.P.R. session using Music Therapy

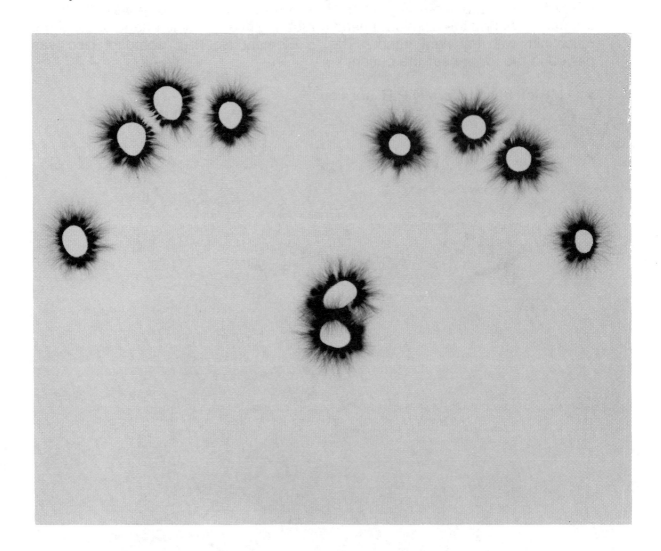

My Right Hand

In summary, by deliberately selecting beneficial belief systems and identities, we are automatically creating the frequencies necessary to keep life flowing and to maintain our balance with the earth. After all, life is a creation. Why not create a life from a selection of your own choices? We must deliberately decide what we want in life and *be* the kind of person capable of creating that life.

References:

Burkhard Heim, Physicist
Jules T. Muheim, Physicist

The Harvard Dictionary of Music

Dr. Fritz Popp, Bio-Physicist and author of "Electromagnetic Bio-Information"; Dr. Wolfgang Ludwig, Diplomat Physicist, Internationally acclaimed inventor and winner of gold medals for his electromagnetic field medical equipment and Dr. Bodo Koehler, MD, Internal Medicine. Dr. Koehler and Dr. Ludwig both developed the "MultiCom" color, sound, gem and laser medical equipment. In Europe, there are Universities which support and fund this research, consequently the research is performed with state of the art technology.

Kirlian Photography was taken at Pantheon Research, Marina Del Rey, Ca.

Chapter 6
The Rhythm Of The Universe
Definitions

Logarithmic:

1. Reckoning, reason and number.   2. The exponent indicating the power to which a fixed number (the base) must be raised to produce a given number.

Chapter 7
Quantic Homeopathy

Every plant or mineral consumed produces not only a physical symptom, but also a mental and emotional symptom. Thus, homeopathic remedies have the ability to affect the entire depiction of a person's physical and emotional make-up. When by using homeopathic methods, you release the identity and belief stored as an electromagnetic charge in the cell's DNA, a re-balancing occurs in the cellular blueprint. The application of homeopathy is unlimited and there are no side effects.

Homeopathy is commonly called, "the energy medicine". Homeopathy is legal, inexpensive and safe. It is globally acclaimed as a profoundly effective medicine, historically dating back to the eighteenth century. Homeopathy is a natural form of medicine, comprised of botanical and mineral sources, including poisonous substances as well. It's important for you to realize that even some organic and botanical substances, have a poisonous effect. This is precisely the reason why homeopathic remedies are diluted and succussed (shaken) to such a degree and for this reason, there are absolutely no residual poisonous effects that remain in a homeopathic remedy. It is truly fascinating to learn that when diluted and succussed into higher and higher potencies eventually there's no physical substance left at all, just pure energy. The once poisonous substance has been rendered completely safe, even for children and can be instrumental in curing many physical and emotional conditions.

The basis for homeopathy stems from the theory, "like cures like", more commonly called the Law of Similars. It was researched and developed by a German doctor, Samuel Hanneman, who wrote: Disease in man is destroyed in a permanent manner by another more powerful force that bears a strong resemblance in it's mode of manifestation. Those substances in a gross material form that produce symptoms will cure those same manifestations in a diluted and dynamized form. Far ahead of his time he was aware that each homeopathic remedy has a corresponding mental symptom. For example, when the remedy Calendula Officinalis, otherwise known as Marigold, is eaten it creates the following mental symptoms, but when diluted and made into a homeopathic remedy it cures these same symptoms. These include: great irritability, being easily frightened, acute hearing, and intense depression. Another remedy, Arsenicum Album, white oxide of metallic arsenic, is used for many physical ailments, like acne, abscess, alcoholism, anemia, and so on. The mental component of Arsenicum Album cures melancholy, anguish, anger with anxiety, restlessness and the sensations of coldness and madness. What actually occurs when a homeopathic remedy is administered? The remedy emits an electromagnetic signal which locates and then adheres to a "similar signal" within the body, thus neutralizing the "similar signal". The "similar signal" that has been located and adhered to is the energy pattern containing the disease. Thus the disease, the identity and the entire energy pattern is dissolved

An important development leading to Dr. Hanneman's remarkable discovery occurred when he first tried to dilute the substances without succussion. This procedure succeeded in reducing the toxicity of the substance, but it also proportionately reduced the therapeutic effect. Then Hanneman experimented with adding kinetic energy into the diluted solutions through shaking or "succussion". The results of this research led to "potentiation," which is a combination of succussion and serial dilution. The critical thing here is the more the substance is succussed and diluted, the higher the potency.

The procedure is as follows: The substance is dissolved in an alcohol/water solution called a tincture. Then one drop of the tincture is diluted into anywhere from 9 to 99 drops of 40% alcohol/water solution. This dilution is then firmly succussed or shaken 100 times. One drop of this dilution is then added to the same amount, 9 to 99 drops of fresh alcohol/water, which is again succussed 100 more times. This process can be continued again and again, with each dilution increasing the therapeutic effect.

The examples given in this chapter on homeopathic remedies and the emotions they address are only a minuscule part of the entire library of information available on the uses of homeopathy.

The hierarchy of treatment that I employ with regard to suggesting homeopathic use is as follows: (1) mental; (2) emotional; (3) physical. The mind stimulates the emotion which is then resisted, creating the physical illness. The emotional and physical levels are symptomatic levels. The physiology of homeopathy, according to the late Dr. Hans Reckweg, MD, indicates that when you take a remedy, it works from the present time backward to conception, and addresses all traumatic incidents connected to the health or emotional issue. If a person takes a homeopathic remedy and does not get results, it's either the wrong remedy or the wrong potency or dosage. Testing with N.P.R. will insure the correct results.

Neuro-Emotional Remedies™

Recent research in psycho-neuroimmunology indicates a direct correlation between stress, emotions and disease and has shown stress has a profound effect on the immune system. As incredible as it may seem, it has also been found that the immune system responds directly and immediately to creative intent and to positive change. This fact inspired my development of 13 Neuro-Emotional Remedies™. The emergence of this new system of healing integrates the ancient theory of acupuncture with it's emotional correlation to meridians, and homeopathy with it's corresponding mental symptoms

The precise combination of homeopathy remedies in each Neuro-Emotional Remedy actually resurfaces and then dissolves the "identity" along with the unconscious cellular memory of traumatic events.

 N.R. Remedies have properties to drain and detoxify the entire energy pattern from the body through the lymphatic system, the urine, the bowels and perspiration. Through researching the formula for N.R. Remedies I discovered that homeopathy works along acupuncture meridian pathways and in conjunction with the immune system. Each ingredient was evaluated and chosen for it's precise emotional and mental correlation to the "Five Element Theory". What evolved was the development of high potency homeopathic remedies with added drainage properties which virtually eliminate homeopathic aggravation. Homeopathic aggravation is a normal aspect of homeopathic treatment and simply put, means, symptoms may get worse before they get better.   However, with the addition of a drainage remedy, homeopathic aggravation can be lessened or virtually eliminated.

Chapter 8
The Transmission Of Epidemics

The brain, nervous system, and cells of every living creature relies on a wireless telecommunication system. As far back as 1918 there have been documented observations of the transmission of plagues and epidemics spreading world wide in as a day or two. These transmissions travel faster than people, birds or insects could ever do in so short a time. It seems clear in both the disharmonic frequency involved and the transference of physical conditions was managed and is maintained through telepathy. This can explain the quick proliferation of AIDS and other so called "contagious disease."

Not only are physical conditions and mental fears spread around the world at "impossible" speeds, but world conditions like faltering economies, political disasters and human tragedies spread like wildfire, due in large part to a plethora of media bombardment. Most of us have experienced the media's broadcast of fear and negativity. These negative belief systems can lower our immune systems if we choose to buy into the negativity. Don't be fearful - pick up your remote and push the "mute" button or change the channel and experience another reality. A helpful way to alleviate this situation might be to consciously neutralize any resistance you may have to the media in general.

You might be asking, "Aren't there some aspects to life we simply have no control over, like gravity for instance?". Yes, we are for the most part bound by gravity. Yet, there are exceptions to the laws of gravity. There have been documented cases of yogi masters levitating in the air. Obviously, they're not bound by mass consciousness limitations. They are capable of experiencing their personal universe as a universe which may or may not include gravity as an absolute. They are not defying the laws of gravity, instead they're showing us other systems of belief which are available and possible. This phenomena may seem inconceivable to us in the context of our own current and cultural belief systems. Evolution calls for a letting go of limitations, which in turn allows for the possibility of an expanded consciousness.

Chapter 9
NeuroPhysical Reprogramming™

How does "Your Emotional DNA" relate to N.P.R.? It's the most efficient tool available in locating core identities that are trapped in the DNA! These identities or energy patterns possess a physical form, which becomes visible when a traditional diagnostic modality called Thermography is utilized. Thermography indicates a visible pattern of hot and cold spots or temperature changes where ever there is inflammation in the body.

N.P.R. is a non-invasive kinesiological method which will quickly and accurately indicate one's current state of well being by locating where resistance is held in the body. Resistance holds an energy pattern in place. N.P.R. is used to test organs, glands, meridians and their corresponding emotions. N.P.R. is as precise as a polygraph test, when the protocol is followed. It's actually quite simple. The muscle being tested, usually the shoulder muscle is selected, is challenged by testing the arm. During the test the arm goes weak when the person tells a lie and remains strong when telling the truth. A lie weakens and the truth either strengthens or shows no change or reaction. The incredible nature of this discovery is that it's method completely by passes the conscious mind, while simultaneously facilitating the focus of attention on selected subjects, topics, times of life or even on specific people.

The definition of Kinesiology, according to Webster's Dictionary is, **"the study of muscles and their movement"**.

I use muscle testing exactly the way a lie detector is used, getting either a **yes** or **no** answer. I will explain this simple technology. The process starts with the client breathing deeply and slowly and stopping the mind so they can feel their emotions. The analytical mind stops. Then muscle testing (Kinesiology), is performed in a way which allows for 100% accuracy. This type of muscle testing works exactly like a lie detector (polygraph) test, but is perhaps even more accurate. The percentage of accuracy depends on the neutrality of the tester or practitioner's perceptions.

First, the practitioner must be in a totally neutral state.   Only in a neutral state will the information gleaned from the client not be influenced by the practitioner.

The next step is to initiate a series of questions to the client while she holds her arm straight out from the body, but also bent back toward the body. For the best results, the client should have no attention on her physical body. The client should be lying down. When the testing is ready to begin, the client's arm will be pushed down by the practitioner while the client pushes against the practitioner's hand. The client tries to prevent her arm from being pushed down. The client then makes a statement and if the statement is true, the arm and muscle will be strong. If the statement is false, the arm and muscle will go weak and the client will not be able to hold her arm up no matter how hard she tries. The false statement registers a weakness in the nervous system and thus the muscle. If we continued the N.P.R. protocol we would soon discover one of the elements in the Five Element Theory is out of balance along with the corresponding emotion. Next there is a series of questions and statements leading to the discovery and complete elimination of causal identities. This technique offers a simple way to do a difficult task, the bypassing of the conscious mind. Once we are linked up to the unconscious nothing can stop the progress. That is, nothing except a session being stopped for some reason. A session can last anywhere from 30 to 90 minutes.

Since your present state of physical health corresponds to your overall emotional state, it's not difficult to find the connection between the two. Based on the Five Element Theory of Acupuncture, N.P.R. is about discovering this connection. Through the use of N.P.R. you'll discover, explore and experience not only your emotions, but your beliefs and identities as well by communicating with your own cellular intelligence.

How quickly can you determine what identity is causing a problem in your life? You can discover numerous sabotaging identities, beliefs and emotions in as little as 5 minutes if you become proficient at this technique. With resistance to feeling the process takes longer. A cellular re-synthesis occurs whenever an identity is eliminated and replaced with a new more desired identity. Many clients say they can feel the re-synthesis occur. An identity is dissolved with the right use, at the right time during the session, of either Neuro-Emotional Remedies™ or one of the music therapy compact discs.

With N.P.R. we are able to learn exactly and immediately what exists on a cellular level. This is truly an incredible opportunity for you to explore and discover what "makes you tick" and what makes you create the things you create in your life.

If you perceive you are not well or not O.K. in some way, there exists an identity and supporting belief which is creating that experience.

Cutting-Edge Research

NeuroPhysical Reprogramming was tested at an independent neurologist's office. A 22 electrode EEG was used on my patients along with advanced computerized biofeedback technology. The biofeedback technology allowed us to monitor 4 additional EEG sites on the occipital lobe of the cranium, in addition to E.M.G. (muscle response), Skin Temperature and Conductance. The sites of measurements on the occipital lobe were specifically chosen to measure responses from the Meta Point leading to the primitive brain and Meta Consciousness. Let me explain. About two years ago I discovered Meta Consciousness and the Meta Point. Both are where old foundation belief systems and identities may be stored, possibly for lifetimes. You know those old patterns and issues that keep popping up and waving a red flag, seemingly impossible to dissolve. These are the old energy patterns which need a super strength industrial technology just to locate them. N.P.R. is that industrial strength technology. Back to the testing. Each N.P.R. session lasted about 30 minutes. The sessions went like this: First, each patient identified the problem and with the help of all the BioFeedback and EEG equipment we determined the most emotionally charged issue. Next, we uncovered all the beliefs systems and identities the patient had regarding the issue. The patient was then guided to begin feeling everything. As the patient maintained a higher state of feeling, either N. R. Remedies or music therapy was introduced. Finally, the patient advised us the charge had been dissolved or been lifted (all other tests also indicated the concurrence of these events). We then ended this part of the sessions by reintroducing the exact same highly charged issues, questions and statements to the patient. There was no charge - no response.

When the patients were feeling a belief, identity or emotion it was clearly seen on the print out of the EEG and my other testing procedures. One of the most amazing and significant aspects of the testing was the use of homeopathy and music therapy. At the time patients were fully feeling their emotions, a few drops of Neuro-Emotional Remedies™ was introduced into the equations by gently placing the drops under the patients tongue with their mouth slightly parted. The next fascinating discovery was when music therapy, instead of the Neuro-Emotional Remedies™, was utilized on a different patient yielding the same results. It was like the energy pattern being intensified by the patient had just dissolved. At the completion of the protocol on the patients, I asked each patient the same initial questions to determine if there was any charge left on their specific topic or issue. With every issue, of which there were quite a few, there was no response indicated on the EEG, E.M.G., G.S.R., and so forth. Interestingly the responses indicated from each patient's data were very similar. Even though the Neuro-Emotional Remedies™ were used on one patient and the "5 Element Healing" C.D., music therapy, on another, the identities and beliefs were dissolved. This research indicated that the correct frequencies of sound or the correct homeopathic remedies work in the same way. They both produce healing vibrations.

But wait, since the old energy pattern is dissolved, there's still an empty space needing to be filled. The patient deliberately and precisely selects a new identity, a champion identity which will manifest and shift their experience.

More About Kinesiology!

Kinesiology, also known as muscle testing, is a system of evaluating and monitoring the normal and abnormal functioning of the nervous system, muscles, organs, glands and other body systems or emotions. The first protocol utilizing muscle testing was developed by Dr. George Goodheart in the early 1960's. His system came to be known as "Applied Kinesiology" and is used extensively by chiropractors and other health professionals worldwide. Other health professionals also made major contributions in the advancement of muscle testing. John Barton, who developed Bio-Kinesiology, who was also the first to connect muscles, tendons, joints, veins, organs and glands to positive and negative words and emotions. Dr. Alan Beardall, who passed on several years ago, researched and developed "Clinical Kinesiology". This is a system of muscle testing incorporating "hand modes" (various finger placements touching acupuncture points and meridians on the hand) into the Doctor's elaborate and extraordinary system of healing. Using "Clinical Kinesiology", you can test an individual for practically anything. After years of practicing many forms of muscle testing, I realized the accuracy of the test depends on the consciousness and neutrality of the practitioner. Most forms of muscle testing could not duplicated. For example if several practitioners tested the same patient one immediately after the other, each practitioner's diagnosis would be different. This observation frustrated me for years. Ultimately the frustration was not in vain, for it lead to the creation of N.P.R.

The validity of muscle testing has been established using various mechanical and electrical machines like the Kinesiometer and the Dynamometer. The Kinesiometer measures the varying electrical impulses in the muscles the same way as an E.K.G., E.C.G. and Polygraph. The Dynamometer records the actual variances in muscle strength. Although machines measure variations in the strength of a muscle, they cannot compare to the sensitivity and versatility achieved through manual testing, as long as the tester stays out of the way and assumes the role of "observer". For some professionals learning to "consistently" stay neutral, detached and out of the way is the most difficult part of my Wellness training.

When a muscle responds to testing using normal strength it has proper nerve stimulation. When a muscle responds to testing with below normal strength this indicates an interference with the normal functioning of the nervous system. We know that specific organs are linked with specific muscles through the complex pathways and neuronal pools of the central nervous system. Energy flow is sequential, starting at the brain and flowing to the cells and back. By testing the strength of certain muscles, information can be learned about organ function. Next, by finding the nutrition, exercise or emotion which will make the muscle test strong again, we can "turn on" the corresponding organ. This results in the body's renewed ability to heal itself.

I have found N.P.R. to be a fascinating and indispensable tool which can detect hidden elements in our belief systems, identities and judgments. Although these hidden elements may be invisible to us, they have the potential to have a tremendously sabotaging effect on our bodies and on our lives.

By the way, you can learn to accurately muscle test **yourself.** I have been told by my students the self-testing protocol of N.P.R. will at the very least eliminate the fear of the unknown.

For the most experienced health practitioner, it takes at the least five 8 hour days to integrate N.P.R. and perform it accurately. The technique takes practice, like playing any instrument or learning a computer program, but once you integrate it you'll have it for life.

Chapter 10
More Transformations

Here are a few more of my case histories and some of those from health professionals who use my techniques and self-empowerment tools with their patients. The healing and transformations were assisted using Neuro-Emotional Remedies™ and/or NeuroPhysical Reprogramming™

The most dramatic experience of my career occurred with the following patient, so much so, that it completely solidified my perspective of healing.

A 23 year old female patient with juvenile diabetes walked into my office one day hoping to get help with her condition, which included the fact she was legally blind. What she didn't count on that first day was, I believed in her ability to heal herself and would empower her to do so as well. When she arrived she was wearing an insulin pump attached to her abdomen. Her skin and hair had a yellowish tint to it. After testing her I discovered she had a kidney dysfunction. She said she was aware of this condition. Then she told me traditional medicine could do nothing else for her. I then thought...what else is she withholding from me? As she desired, I saw her once or twice a week for the next three months. During this time it was revealed to me she had an emotionally abusive childhood with several traumatic events taking place causing her to unconsciously create illness and self-destruction. She also had a recreational drug history, being on many medications at the same time. Yet, I saw a spark in her eye that convinced me she was going to heal herself, even after she was hospitalized with kidney failure as a result of taking heavy drugs twice during the duration of our association.

The scenario went like this: After three months of my working with her, she was taken off her insulin pump it was no longer required. At my request, her MD put her on human insulin, instead of the insulin from pigs. She started feeling the best she had in years and actually got a job for the first time in her life. She reported back to me even her vision was better. (Before this time, I thought once you were legally blind, that was it - you were destined for a life of blindness.) Unfortunately, things were going too well for her. According to the Five Element Theory of Acupuncture, the feeling of being overwhelmed with excessive joy affects the heart and is associated with the Fire element. She took recreational drugs again resulting in her hospitalization. I saw her daily in the hospital. Her frail body was yellow and swollen. Her physician told her it was hopeless, she would surely die due to kidney failure. Her kidney function was roughly 1 to 2 percent of normal and the doctor reported dialysis would not work. I asked to be alone with her. We remained alone for more than an hour or two. Time seemed to stop. She was very still. However, I felt this flow of love and communication coming through me which had to be expressed. I told her the doctor isn't God. I told her he had nothing to do with her decision to live or die and she could decide to live and heal herself. I also told her it was O.K. to die, that I would stay with her and help her in her transition. I told her to just decide on her own. To be in her power and make whatever she desired happen. She spoke after more than an hour or so. She said, "But my body is such a mess." I told her I didn't see it that way, I experienced her being spiritually ready to reverse this condition - if she chose! I observed there was a gray cloud in the room just over her head which smelled moldy and musty. I told her I could see this gray cloud over her and she needed to make a decision --- NOW. I then asked her if she 'd made a decision and if so what was her decision. If it hadn't been for the fact I had left my body, (To become a detached observer, so I wouldn't interfere with her process or decision.) I would have been in shock, probably held my breath and choked. She said " Yes....I want to live". At that moment the gray cloud I was watching vanished with a puff of smoke, like a magic trick of some kind. The musty odor was gone, too. She smiled and her cheeks started turning a pinkish color. I then knew she'd turned the corner. I asked her what she wanted now. She said "Send the doctor in." and proceeded to advise her physician she wanted to leave the hospital because she was going to recover. He rebutted that remark. She insisted and told him he had no right to pass his beliefs to her and that he was not God. He apologized to her and she was out of the hospital in less than two weeks.

I continued working with her until she was well enough to control her own life. Eventually she moved to another part of the country where she began writing a book and living with her husband. Five or six years later I received a phone call from a friend of hers who told me the woman had recovered, but then one day while riding the bus she suddenly dropped dead of a heart attack. Despite the fact there was no history of heart problems in her past. My point of view is, after the episode in the hospital and her subsequent recovery she may again have experienced excessive joy as before. Only this time it caused a heart attack. I believe she left once she completed her mission here and fully experienced her power to heal herself. Then, *pouf*, she left her body! It never ceases to amaze me how choices we make actually manifest into reality. She was probably around 31 or 32 years old. Needless to say, this relationship was a gift to me. It provided me with the enthusiasm and passion I continue to feel for my life and work. I only wish I had discovered N.P.R. during this time so I could have helped her even more.

♦

A female patient, age 45, reported during her first office visit, she'd suffered from asthma for 11 years, ever since the birth of her son. Employing NeuroPhysical Reprogramming we discovered pent up grief, anger, and resentment relating to the way doctors treated her before and during her delivery. We peeled off the layers of identities using the appropriate remedies for the lung, liver, and gallbladder. Afterwards her breathing greatly improved. During the second visit her breathing and lung capacity normalized and I sent her home with the three remedies mentioned above and to be taken as directed. The cause of the condition was released.

♦

A female patient, age 42, had a muscular weakness in her right foot and ankle for years causing her to limp, even when using a cane. Through NeuroPhysical Reprogramming, we found her condition had begun after she and her husband started going dancing. She discovered she resented him because he enjoyed dancing with other women. This indicated low-self esteem (pancreas), along with the beliefs "she had to do what her husband wanted her to do", and "he is the man and in control." Using my protocol she eliminated the identity, belief, and emotion (low self-esteem), and left the office that day *without relying on her cane to walk* . She continued for three more visits to work on other life conditions and relationships. She successfully eliminated the cause of her condition.

♦

A male, age 35, who was self-employed as an actor and screenwriter complained of various physical conditions which lead to a mild paranoia about his health and his appearance. After 4 sessions of N.P.R. he discovered much of the unhappiness and anger he felt was due to his being repeatedly cast theatrically as a rapist or other violent character. In other words, he never dropped the identities he assumed for his acting roles. After this realization, he experienced a major shift in his outlook and in addition began to perceive his appearance differently. Once he told me he actually felt his facial bones moving after one of our sessions. I also observed a physical change, a softening, in his appearance and facial structure. His appearance changed radically, from long curly locks to a clean short haircut. He even dressed differently. Our sessions continued until he stopped creating physical conditions and was well on the road to success in his life. In fact he learned to test himself using my protocol so he no longer needed to come in for sessions. He went on to use the self-testing tools to create and realize his dream of writing and acting in films.

◆

A doctor from Missouri wrote the following case history:
I want to thank you for teaching me about Neuro-Emotional Remedies™. and N.P.R. It has allowed me to get to the root of my clients' health problems. A good example is my best friend who happens to be a chiropractor. He had a bad knee for 20 years that kept him from doing some of the martial art forms that we study together. I asked him if I could help. In five minutes we cleared out the problem and he has not experienced pain in his knee since. Now he can do the forms with no trouble at all. Thanks.

◆

A doctor from Arizona wrote the following testimonial and case history:
Mr. B., a 50 year old Caucasian male, was diagnosed with Multiple Myeloma, a plasma cell, and therefore an immune system cell cancer, which in traditional medical circles, is believed to be fatal within a few years, even with chemotherapy. So he turned to the holistic medical circuit for help and became a patient of a colleague of mine, an holistic and homeopathic physician. This colleague helped him greatly to rebuild his physical energy and balance. However, because he is aware that the root cause for this, or any other illness, is not primarily physical, he sent Ed to me for identification and release of these mental and emotional causative factors.

We found that Ed had a rather difficult childhood. He never knew his father and was raised by his mother in a rather harsh setting where there was little space for nurturing. Consequently, his self-esteem was neither very strong nor stable. In his adult life he worked himself up to becoming the manager in a clothing store, a well-paid position in which he found himself to be capable and effective. Accordingly, he felt good about himself. The tide turned when his boss's wife decided to get involved with the store. John had to first educate her about what was going the business. Then and rather soon, she decided she was ready to take charge and reduced Ed to a seemingly meaningless part of the store inventory. Understandably this was more than he could bear. Within two years, he was diagnosed with cancer.

He tested positive for the remedies for the lungs (grief), the heart (shock and overwhelmed, no joy), the liver and gall-bladder (anger and resentment), the kidneys (worry and fear), and the spleen / pancreas (low self-esteem, having no power or control).

Having worked with him on a weekly basis for about six week, helping him to identify and release his intense bottled-up emotions. His anger and resentment toward his ex-boss's wife being the strongest one, he is now feeling much better, more peaceful, and aware he is indeed turning the emotional roller-coaster around which led to his cancer. This can result in a complete healing. The Neuro-Emotional Remedies™ have in my experience, as in this case as well as in many others, proven to be a powerful tool to release intense negative emotional charges and belief systems, already resulting in physical illness. They deserve to be worked on by any holistic practitioner who is aware of the truth: that we need to start focusing and much more than we have so far, on healing the mind — as it is always the mind that makes the body sick or well. Thank you, Theresa, for your inspired gift of the healing arts.

◆

Another medical doctor from Arizona wrote the following case history:
A female:
Symptoms: Pain in gallbladder area, severe at times. Pains in both the lower right and left sides with diarrhea or irregular bowels. Chronic fatigue and head "fog".
Diagnosis: After a thorough G.I. Series the diagnosis was Diverticulosis and irritable bowl.
The correct Neuro-Emotional Remedies™ were prescribed.
Results: After 2 weeks there was less "fog" in her head and the pain in her gallbladder began to subside. After 4 weeks, practically no diarrhea, very little pain and a great increase in physical endurance and stamina.

One Of My Favorite Patients
Once Said......

Doctor Dale...

I Am Trying To Get Pregnant..... But --

I Don't Want To Have Sex
With My Husband..

Can You Tell Me Why I Can't Get
Pregnant?

Chapter 11
Five Element Theory and Emotions

The Chinese philosophical theory of the Five Elements can be traced back 4000 years before Christ. It is a diagnostic and a treatment modality that is very accurate. It invites individuals to take responsibility for the creation of their physical conditions by associating specific emotions to various organs and glands in the body.

The Five Element Theory also demonstrates that every acupuncture meridian (energy channel) within the body has a corresponding emotion. In turn, each resisted emotion emits a frequency which is stored in its specifc organ and is detectable through Kinesiology (muscle testing). For example, the liver meridian, and the liver itself, may be weakened when a person resists feeling anger. The **resisted** emotion actually becomes <u>stuck</u> in that organ until it is experienced and then dissolved.

The five elements are: **WOOD, FIRE, EARTH, METAL** and **WATER**. The elements are kept under control by two basic forces referred to as: CREATION AND DISCREATION.

Each element has a corresponding season, taste, color, odor, sound, physical and emotional symptom along with other distinct correlations.

The book, "Five elements and Ten Stems" by Kiiko Matsumoto and Stephen Birch documents the development of the Chinese Five Element Theory. One aspect of this ancient theory is the concept of Yin and Yang. Through this concept the Chinese view becomes the very essence of their life, emotions and environment.

Very simply, Yang, the energy of heaven, relates to each aspect of The Five Elements. Whereas, Yin, the energy of earth, corresponds to the twelve main acupuncture meridians. The overall influence of heaven and earth on the body provides the basis for the Chinese Five Element Theory.

Another aspect to the Yin and Yang theory is food combining. In my cookbook, "Biotic Mac Slow Foods", I describe the different degrees of Yin and Yang foods. In the book specific guidelines for recognizing Yin and Yang foods are explained. Basically, foods that are Yin are grown above the ground. That means the higher above the earth the vegetables are grown the more Yin exists within. Yang, on the other hand, describes all foods grown deep in the earth, such as root vegetable.

By observing **Chart 1, The Five Elements**, you can easily see how the elements influence one another. Here are three important principles for your exploration:

1. Within each circle of the chart there are two or more organs or glands and a number which relates to the corresponding Neuro-Emotional Remedy. The organs and glands in the same circle are energetically related by energy channels called acupuncture meridians.

2. When you are exploring a physical condition, a pain or a sensation, like say in the gallbladder, you may find the correct emotion and belief related to the condition in the other organ in that circle, in this case being the liver.

3. The physical condition does not always stay stationary in the same organ manifesting the symptoms.

Energy Patterns Can Relocate

The arrows on the Five Elements Chart point from one element to another. There are also arrows within the same element. The arrows within the same element are indicative of a transference of the identity's energy pattern from one organ to another within the same element. For example, the Water Element contains two meridians and two organs; the kidney and the bladder. A physical condition that starts in one organ, let's say the kidney can affect the bladder and visa versa. On the other hand, the arrows pointing to different elements indicate that one element may be affecting other elements. For example, a liver condition (Wood element) that is not handled can affect the heart (circulation) or endocrine system, both located in the Fire element. This would explain why a liver condition called hepatitis can adversely affect the heart. In the same way anger is related to the liver and if the belief that keeps stimulating anger by attracting events and situations is resisted and not eliminated, the resisted frequency of anger would stay in the liver until released. Once released it might flow to the heart, causing symptoms there.

What happens when you surgically remove an organ? From an acupuncture viewpoint, if a person was to have a malfunctioning organ surgically removed, the stored energy pattern containing the resisted emotion and identity, would continue to stay stuck in the same area of the body or travel to a corresponding meridian and organ. You can not surgically remove the cause of your illness. The identity just relocates itself in another organ and meridian.

I have seen thousands of patients who tried to heal from one problem after another. It seems as though when one issue or illness cleared up -- another one manifested. Some came to me seeking help after exploring many different holistic therapies -- to no avail. They were continuously creating either the same condition with lesser symptoms or different conditions. After tracking the condition using N.P.R. I was amazed at the accuracy of this ancient theory of healing.

You may find it easy to take a drug, herbal remedy, or vitamins for a physical symptom. You are looking for something to "make it better" and take the pain away. You may even be looking for someone else to take the pain away by loving you. My viewpoint is that when you continuously rely on something outside yourself to "make it better", you deprive yourself of the opportunity to experience control of your destiny.

No matter how hard you are "trying" to get well or how much you "really want to get well", there is one thing that will prevent your healing. If you desired the identity at some point in your life, that desire needs to be acknowledged and experienced. If the desire is never acknowledged, then the decision and the identity will continue to exist at the core of the illness or life condition. First of all *trying* implies resistance -- *doing* -- creates a flow. The truth is at a particular point in your life some aspect of the identity and its decision was desired.

See **Chart 2** for the correlation between Neuro-Emotional Remedies and The Five Element Theory.

References:

Diane M. Connelly, Ph.D., MAC. *The Law of the Five Elements*

Kiiko Matsumoto and Stephen Birch. *Five Elements and Ten Stems*

Dr. Franz Morrell, MD. (Germany). *Mora Therapy and the Five Elements*

Chart 1
FIVE ELEMENTS

©1994 Theresa Dale, N.D.

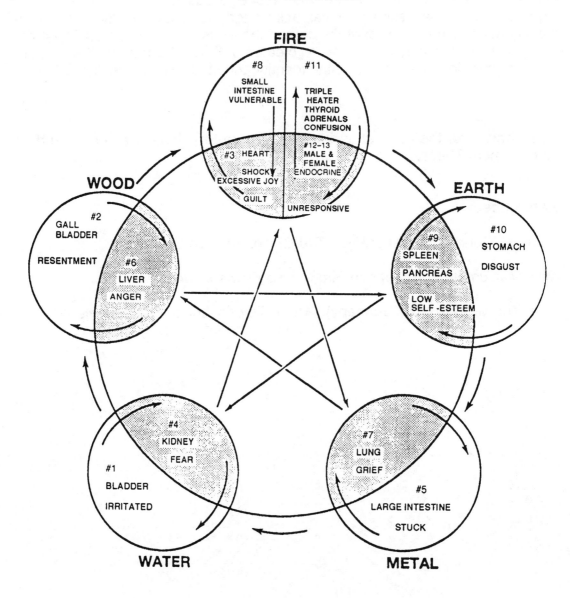

Arrows show energetic pattern of emotion flowing
from organ to organ — element to element

Chart 2
Neuro-Emotional Remedies™ and The Five Element Theory

Fire Element

N.R.	Organ or Gland	Emotion
#3.	Heart	Shock or Trauma / Excessive Joy / Guilt
#8.	Small Intestine	Vulnerable
#11.	Thyroid-Adrenals Glands	Confusion
#12.	Male Endocrine System	Unresponsive or Numb
#13.	Female Endocrine System	Unresponsive or Numb

Earth Element

#9.	Spleen / Pancreas	Low Self Esteem
#10.	Stomach	Despair or Disgust

Metal Element

#5.	Large Intestines	Feeling Stuck
#7.	Lung	Grief

Water Element

#1.	Bladder	Irritated
#4.	Kidney	Fear

Wood Element

#2.	Gall Bladder	Resentment
#6	Liver	Anger

Chapter 12
Therapeutic Fasting

If your goal is enlightenment then this detoxification procedure will speed you on your journey. It is of vital importance to detoxify and undo the layers of emotional and chemical sludge accumulated since birth. The method of fasting in this chapter is a safe and effective tool that will help you make way for new identities that can better serve your highest purpose. You will experience a lightness and clarity that will not only assist you in the integration of the "new you", but will take years off your biological age.

Fasting is as old as the history of man. It is a method used in "Naturopathy" to procure new vitality. However paradoxical it seems, voluntary fasting should not be confused with suffering from hunger.

The therapeutic value of fasting has been known for centuries. A promising rediscovery of fasting was made in 1878 when the American physician Dr. Dewey cured a typhoid patient with a 35 day fasting cure. Another American physician, Dr. Tanner, practiced fasting over a period of 40 days in order to heal himself of digestive troubles. The German-Russian physician Dr. von Seeland practiced fasting in 1887 and discovered that his body and his nervous system both responded favorably.

Names like Dr. Adolf Masyer, Dr. Meller, Dr. Riedlin and Dr. Kapferer belong to the long line of famous fasting therapists. The master of fasting therapy in Germany is Dr. Otto Buchingersen. In 1918, as a 40-year old major general in the medical corps of the marines, he fell ill with chronic arthritis. He was labeled "incurable" in the opinion of classical medicine. So this father of four was quickly ushered into retirement. His situation was desperate. Finally, he tried a fasting cure and allowed himself water only. This proved to be the powerful answer. He was permanently and forever freed from his health condition. Maybe it was the fast, or perhaps his desperately held strong belief, that worked the cure. Regardless, the results were irrefutable. Much to the benefit of mankind the biological effects of fasting were rediscovered and applied by Dr. Otto Buchingersen. The doctor was able to prove once again that fasting can be a valuable tool for the building of health.

Again, let me make something clear; Fasting and suffering from hunger are two very different things. You do not have to buy into or create suffering from constant dieting. If you choose to explore the fast outlined in this chapter, do it only temporarily and continue to live a healthy, normal lifestyle, without any fear or paranoia about the food you eat.

Time and again this diet is confused with slimming or the zero-diet. These, and similar measures, serve the principle goal of losing weight. At first glance the zero-diet resembles the fasting cure when practiced under exacting conditions and under constant supervision, but the conditions under which the two fasts are practiced are actually quite different. The zero-diet is recommended for people who believe they have an acute illness. The person **must not work during the fast,** (another excuse to play hooky) and should rest whenever possible. In Europe, curative fasting therapy is practiced in the quiet atmosphere of a special clinic and in the company of others pursuing the same goal. This "group therapy", in pleasant surroundings, encourages self-contemplation and mental "purging".

Fasting on one's own can be done safely and effectively if a person adheres to the fast and allows the body to rid itself of stored toxins in organs, systems, glands and, of course, body fat. The survivor of a pure water fast resembles his or her former self in appearance only. He or she is like new, except for their higher self, which always remains pure and untouched.

Fasting on water allows all digestive processes to cease during the fast and in turn let's the organs rest and rid themselves of stored toxins. It is an extreme method, but in some cases it is the best method. Fasting on vegetable broth, water, and herbal tea is more tolerable for many because it allows a person to fast while working. The vegetable broth provides an adequate electrolyte balance (sodium, potassium, chloride). This is quite helpful and actually quite essential if you want to continue living here on Earth for any length of time. (A good sense of humor can also help you sail through a fast.)

For a few days at the beginning of the fast a certain quantity of nutrients and combustibles (Sounds like we're going to be blowing something up doesn't it!) are still available in the various deposits. The glycogen stored in the liver and the substances dissolved in the blood can nourish the body in the usual manner for another three days. At this stage all metabolic processes are reduced to a minimum. Once these deposits are depleted, the organism switches to its "emergency supply". In order to maintain the nitrogen balance, the fat deposits must be used. For this utilization to occur, a complete change of metabolism is necessary. In addition, all ways of mobilizing protein reserves must be employed.

Free protein can be found in substances and compounds, which under normal circumstances serve parasitic functions within the organism. All toxic deposits are now used up very quickly by virtue of the body's use of its "emergency supply". All waste and noxious compounds that cannot be used up in this manner are discharged by the newly activated "waste removal mechanism". Foreign substances are also eliminated in this manner.

The result? Any accumulated physical toxic matter or neuro-toxin is sloughed off. After depletion of fat in the cells, considerable weight is lost and the storage cells shrink, especially in the first few days. Please note that a steady weight loss throughout the fast does not occur. Instead, in the first week, the person loses up to two pounds per day; in the second week, only one pound per day; in the third week, half a pound at the most; and in the fourth he will lose a mere quarter of a pound per day. Weigh yourself and observe the fascinating and marvelous results.

The timing for "breaking" the fast and the subsequent return to a normal diet are important in the lasting effect of a fasting cure. The person who has finished a fast must slowly readapt to a normal eating regimen with specific dietary guidance. No matter how bad one feels at the beginning, middle or end of the fast, it is routinely reported most people feel "brand new", healthier, stronger, fresher, and more "fit" by the time the fast is completed. The most encouraging thing is that the newly achieved vitality has a lasting effect, if the person chooses wisely.

Very few side effects have been reported from fasting, only a normal period of detoxification. (You can handle this part, it's a piece of cake!) We have already discussed a few of the positive changes an individual is entitled to expect. The advantages to fasting for the organs are that with the smaller work load they are allowed to rest during the fast. Most importantly the digestive organs are allowed to rest and heal. Depriving the metabolism of any food supply forces it to fall back on the body's accumulated reserves and metabolic waste in order to survive. This "eating up" of reserves and waste leads to a purification of the whole body quickly and more securely than any other method of natural treatment.

Fasting has proven to be surprisingly successful in so-called "civilization body conditions". Unfortunately, rapid weight loss is often the only goal some hope to achieve by fasting. This misses an important benefit, because fasting not only provokes a reduction of the body's substances, it also regulates disturbed hormonal functions. Many are surprised and delighted to find that a three or four week therapy results not only in the loss of pounds, but also in the normalization of long standing conditions. Even a two week course of fasting with herbal broth will often achieve incredible results.

During fasting, substances like drugs, chemicals and metabolic waste products are eliminated through the urine and the bowels. This elimination may produce symptoms in people who believe they are "ill", but usually these symptoms only indicate varying signs of toxicity. In these cases the fast can be eased or shortened when the sensations become too uncomfortable.

The Fast

Healthful benefits can be gained for working individuals by fasting for a period of one to two weeks and for those without a hectic schedule, fasting for a period of three to four weeks. If you prefer to fast for 3 to 4 weeks, I would suggest you consider including herbal broth, almond milk, herbal teas -- and, of course, plenty of water.

The immediate benefits of fasting are:
- Blood Pressure normalization
- Weight Loss
- Detoxification
- Looking and feeling younger
- Increased energy -- feeling lighter

If one continues with a dietary regime of healthy whole foods the long term effects on the body are as follows:

- More control over weight
- Balanced metabolism, including normalized blood sugar
- because the fasting gives the pancreas a rest
- A noticeable difference in mental clarity
- A better handle on the emotional realm
- Normal eliminations

During the fast one should not engage in strenuous sports activities. However, yoga, stretching or walking can all be good ideas. The fast below can be safely followed for a 7 or 14 day period. For some, the longer the better, because the body only begins to detoxify after three or four days.

An important note: For the **first two days** of the fast some experience their best results from eating only fruit, and drinking herbal teas and water. One tablespoon of honey can be a treat once or twice daily. Bee propolis is a very helpful addition, because it contains vitamins and other good stuff. It is helpful to drink herbal teas made with pure water. A minimum of eight 8 oz. glasses of should be consumed daily throughout the fast. Some health practitioners recommend distilled water and some recommend pure mineral water. Either way, a helpful guideline to follow is: When you get hungry, **DRINK, DRINK, DRINK**.

Some clinics recommend a very warm hot water bottle set on a thin towel be placed over the liver, on the right side of the body for 15 minutes after each meal. If this is not possible two times daily would be fine. This helps stimulate the liver to detoxify.

Breakfast

Almond Milk (8 oz)
or SOYA yogurt Blueberry or Apple or Papaya

Lunch
Two cups of Biehler's Broth (see Recipe)

Dinner
Two cups of Biehler's Broth AND an 8 oz. glass of carrot juice

Teas To Drink While Fasting

(You may combine the following teas or use them singularly)
Hibiscus
Linden Flower
Uva Ursi
Comfrey
Chamomile

Pre-Fasting

The pre-fasting period consists of fruit only and serves the purpose of an intestinal purge. This helps remove the waste lodged in the pockets and folds of the large intestines. The first three days of the fast can produce normal detoxification symptoms like headaches or weakness. This usually passes within 24 hours.

If you already have low blood pressure it will usually drop lower during the fast. For example, if your blood pressure is normally 120 over 80, during a fast it can go down to as low as 90 over 60. If you prefer, you can monitor your blood pressure. If feelings of weakness occur during the fast, add some extra soy yogurt, drink more soup or almond milk and at any time you may decide to slowly and gently come off the fast.

If you decide to take multi-vitamins and vitamin C during the fast, you may want to consider taking them in liquid form so your body does not have to break them down.

Ending The Fast

The ending the fast is just as important as the beginning.

This is of most importance because you want to end your fast in a way so that your body can slowly start re-adjusting to solid foods. A regime you might like to follow is as follows:

Day 1

Breakfast

The first day after the end of your fast eat natural, organic apple sauce (no whole fruit) and soy yogurt for breakfast. If soy yogurt is not available where you live, you might want to substitute a protein shake (make with vegetable protein powder and without white sugar or milk products).

Lunch

Lunch should consist of two cups of Beihler's Broth.

Dinner

Dinner should consist of 2 cups of any homemade vegetable soup (no salt) add a little brown rice to the broth.

Continue tea and water intake.

Day 2

Breakfast

The second day after the fast have almond milk for breakfast, followed by one cup of unsweetened Museli with soy milk or organic apple juice.

Lunch

Biehler's Broth with Brown rice and one small piece of Broiled or Grilled Swordfish

Dinner

Steamed string beans and zucchini squash

FOR THE REST OF THE WEEK EAT VERY LIGHTLY

Note: 1 Tsp. of Bernard Jensen's Quik Sip, Bragg's Liquid Aminos, or Tamari Sauce may be used as a salt or seasoning substitute.

On rare occasions, leg cramps may occur during the fast. This is usually from an electrolyte imbalance. Drinking enough of the Biehler's broth and water will correct this situation.

Recipes for Almond Milk and Biehler's Broth

Biehler's Broth: Combine equal amounts of celery, parsley, zucchini, and string beans.

Soak veggies in a sink-full of water and use a natural solution for cleaning the pesticides and parasites.

Steam veggies, then place in blender with pure water. You may puree or finely chop the mixture. You may add fresh garlic and a little Quik-Sip to taste. Heat, DO NOT BOIL.

Eat or drink this broth two to three times daily. It will help you to detoxify while balancing your electrolytes.

Almond Milk

Soak organic almonds over night, then put in blender with pure water and 1 tsp. of barley malt syrup. Blend to the consistency of milk.

Basic Needs Of The Human Body

Just as each person is biochemically individual, a person may have individual needs.

1. Drink eight to nine 8-oz glasses of water daily.
2. Protein and amino acids are necessary, especially if the body does not handle stress well or is exercised insufficiently.
3. Exercise is essential for the body. It is important for the distribution of nutrients and detoxification from stress.
4. The body needs touch, care, and nurturing.
5. Vitamins A, B, C, minerals and Vitamin E are all helpful if a body is active and expends a lot of energy exercising or "processing". (Resistance uses up many nutrients, including minerals, B-vitamins and vitamin C). The body does not

manufacture Vitamin C so it is essential to take 1000 to 3000 mg per day of a buffered or neutral form of Vitamin C. Free-form amino acids are essential if you often work out.

6. Maintain a properly functioning digestive system by eating slowly and taking digestive enzymes when necessary. Although all the nutritional textbooks say that after a certain age your body stops producing Hydrochloric Acid, this is not necessarily true. Your digestive system will greatly improve when you handle your stress by doing the exercises at the end of this book.

7. Eat vegetables. Steamed veggies or fresh vegetable juice is great medicine for any body.

God Created Time

So Everything

Wouldn't Happen At Once!

Chapter 13
Reality Shifting Exercises

The following exercises will gently guide you to many discoveries about yourself and your universe. You may use these exercises as many times as you wish to uncover new layers of beliefs and identities.

Remember, feel everything revealed to you and enjoy being an explorer.

Theresa Dale

Using Reality Shifting Exercises!

When you are Feeling	Exercise
moody	BLISS
lethargic	ATTENTION & ALIGNMENT
down in the dumps	SHIFTING REALITY
mega depressed	BLISS, SHIFTING REALITY
going ballistic	BLISS, ATTENTION & ALIGNMENT
constantly irritated or pissed off	AWARENESS
fearful	BLISS, SHIFTING REALITY
angry	SHIFTING REALITY, BLISS
you want to fire your whole office staff	BLISS; AWARENESS ATTENTION & ALIGNMENT
like a rat	ATTENTION & ALIGNMENT
your not good enough	BLISS
you want to check out	BLISS; AWARENESS, ATTENTION AND ALIGNMENT

you want to kill your mother in law	BLISS, ATTENTION & ALIGNMENT
confusion about who you are	SELF-AWARENESS SURVEY; SHIFTING REALITY
paranoid about everything	AWARENESS
going mental	BLISS
overwhelmed	BLISS, ATTENTION & ALIGNMENT
underwhelmed	BLISS, SHIFTING REALITY
you have a huge creative block	SELF-AWARENESS SHIFTING REALITY

Self-Awareness Survey

The following survey will make you aware of the feelings you **resist**. Each feeling or emotion is grouped in their element, according to the "Five Element Theory of Acupuncture":

What percentage of time in a week are you **resisting** feeling?

Fire Element	**% of Time**
vulnerable	_____
confused	_____
unresponsive	_____
guilt	_____
in shock / trauma	_____
excessive joy / overwhelmed	_____

Earth Element	
low self-esteem	_____
disgust	_____
despair	
	_____

Metal Element	
stuck	_____
grief	
	_____

Water Element

fear   _____
irritated   _____

Wood Element

angry / rage   _____
resentment   _____

The Bliss Exercise

There is an ancient wisdom many seek to experience. This wisdom is silent and lies in the space occurring when you stop the mind. When you stop your mind you no longer resist anything, you no longer desire anything, you are in a clear and empty space -- a blissful nothingness. This exercise will stop the mind in minutes.

First, ensure the best results possible by breathing deeply - in through your nose and out through your mouth. Breathe **s l o w** deep connected breaths. A forced inhalation and a **s l o w** exhalation, now connect this to the next inhalation and exhalation. Breathe deeply in this manner throughout the entire exercise to assist in quieting your mind.

1.   Continue breathing deeply and slowly while you look around your environment. Observe the form or outline of each person or thing and in one second, pull the form into your heart. It only takes one second to place a form into your heart. But, If you stop to stare and analyze a form, you will be back in your head in a moment. Very quickly take the outline or form of objects, people, trees, flowers and even bugs, into your heart. If you want to experience BLISS continue this exercise for 15 minutes to 1/2 hour per day. The effects of this exercise are cumulative.

2. If you have the "5 Element Healing" or "Synchrony" Compact Discs play any of the instrumental selections. Following the instructions above in step 1, notice the form of each note you are listening to and take each note into your heart as quickly as possible, one by one. As a new note emerges, take it quickly into your heart and let go of the previous note. The notes in the past do not exist anymore, let them go and make space for the next new note and its form. This is a great exercise in letting go of the past and assists you in feeling inner peace by stopping the mind. You can try this exercise with any accoustic instrumental selection.

Shifting Any Reality

To eliminate beliefs limiting our experience, we must first quiet our minds. Take a few deep breaths to oxygenate your cells. Close your eyes and breathe deeply and slowly. Know that you are always in control of your experience and allow yourself to feel totally safe. Let me to take you on a little emotional journey...Remember a time when you felt *emotional darkness*. Imagine it. Now shift that feeling into your body. Feel the sensation. Decide this feeling, *emotional darkness*, is a "bad" feeling. Experience this feeling and sensation. Now, change your mind and experience the emotional darkness as a *good* thing. Embrace it. Feel it in every cell of your body. Feel it fully.

You can see how labeling your feelings in new ways can shift your viewpoint and subsequently change your reality.

Continuing the journey... remember a time when you felt *the power of love* for someone, someone you wanted to heal, to love, to support. Embrace it. Feel it in your body. Breathe deeply. Now, feel that *power of love* and direct it towards yourself. Take it in. Embrace it and make it yours.

Breathing deeply helps you explore beliefs. Deliberately decide, *"life is difficult;"*, embrace the sensation, take it inside yourself. Now decide that this belief, *"life is difficult"*, is "serious". Feel the sensation of life as "serious." Embrace the seriousness of the belief. Now, change your mind and deliberately decide to find this belief "silly". Feel it as silly. Feel it in every cell of your body. Continue breathing deeply and slowly. Now experience another belief, one that you might ordinarily resist feeling. That's exactly why we are going to embrace it now. Experience the belief that you are "*a victim*". Explore the belief that you are *a victim*...Embrace the feeling in your body. Now decide to change that belief and reality. Experience being *"a powerful creator of joy and happiness in the world"*. Embrace this belief, feel it in every cell of your body, right down to your toes.

You can see how easily "reality" can be changed. If you can *feel* it, you can *have* it. Let go of the limitations of feeling what you want. What if everyone in the world knew they could experience a new reality this easily? What would be created by mass consciousness then? You will observe from doing these exercises that *you* decide how to feel about everything. Your decisions create your experiences. Life, health, happiness or emotional darkness, it's all your choice, is it not? Now, deliberately decide that *"life is a joyous adventure"* and experience it that way! Go ahead, "feel" your personal power to decide. Embrace the belief that *"life is a joyous adventure",* and make it yours. But remember, in order to manifest any goal, you must be in 100% alignment with the goal itself.

Attention And Alignment Exercise

Is your attention in your life on your physical body? If so, that's an excellent way to limit your creative energy. Focusing on resisting every aspect of your body, like the way you look, smell, an ache, a pain or how about being fearful that getting some physical illness will diminish your potential. If you still wonder why you have not created your ideal relationship, prosperousness, or a mission in your life, you might discover you're expending enormous amounts of energy on other things. Like resisting experience or continuously judging yourself and your life.

The following is an exercise that demonstrates the above: Place all of your attention on your physical body; the ways you look, your hair, your skin, an ache, a pain or the way you are feeling. Do this for about two minutes.

Now, shift that reality by focusing all of your attention on another person and observe them. Notice their features and clothes the way a child would. Notice if any judgments come into your awareness. If so, keep observing them until the judgments fade.

Now, put all of your attention on that person and communicate with them... while you are thinking about yourself.

Ah ha! You cannot put all of your attention in two places, in this case trying to communicate with someone else while you are still thinking about yourself or your body. Yet, often we try to do just this. Many times we want to manifest something, but we do not have our attention available. The result is we fail to get what we want.

Where does our creative intention go when we are not living in the moment? Are you going to sacrifice the present because you are focusing on a future that is unknown? One thing's for sure, our dreams can be available to us here and now. The mind must stop for the intuition and the creative process to begin. Try this exercise to still your mind. Put your attention on your thoughts until your mind stops, then immediately close your eyes. Now, count backwards from

1000 in increments of 3. For example: 1000, 997, 994, etc., until your mind stops and you feel relaxed. From the diaphragm, breathe in through your nose and push the air out of your mouth in slow connected breaths. While you are breathing, feel the different parts of your body without touching them. For example, feel your foot without touching your foot. Start at your toes and work your way up your body.

Alignment

When your 100% aligned with a decision or goal, you will be able to manifest that goal. If even a minuscule part of you has doubt or is unaligned you will be unable to create your goal. Every doubt you feel is either produced by an identity or by constantly focusing your attention on yourself. For instance, let's say you decide to create great health for yourself. If after making this decision you become 100% aligned with the decision, you will be able to create and experience great health. You will be compelled to take a quantum leap into your new reality. Experience and feel it as though it were yours -- now.

You are capable of experiencing your life the way you want, but only if you *know* what you want to experience. Once again you will feel the power you were born with so long ago. You can effortlessly reshape your entire life. Begin by unconditionally believing you *can* do all of these things. Then be 100% aligned with what you want to create and the way you want it created. This is not mind control. It's employing an ability you were born with as a child, before the adults got a hold of you, an innate sense of worth. Trusting and listening to your intuition will carry you over any rough spots to victory. If you want to be ageless, reshape your belief system about aging and eliminate any identities not serving you. This will reflect into direct experience, with "magical" results.

Let's take a look at beliefs you have which are unaligned with your goals, thereby keeping you from achieving your goals. For example, you may feel certain you want perfect health, yet you create one illness after another. Maybe you find yourself with a disease for the first time in your life. Regardless, in both cases you have an invisible, cellular, unaligned belief, serving an identity working against your goal of perfect health. This identity will cause you to see and experience life through its eyes.

Alignment is essential in the manifestation of goals. Are you 100% aligned with your goals? For example, If 99% of you wants something and 1% (an identity) secretly does not, guess what will happen? Your goals will not manifest the way you want. It's true many of these unaligned beliefs are invisible to you, but that does not mean they are not creating visible results.

You may be projecting your identities to every person you meet. Take a good look at your world and observe how people respond to you and your identities.

Alignment Exercise

1. Affirm the goal you desire by putting it as a statement in the present tense. For example; I am totally healthy. I have all the money I need. I have my perfect relationship. And so on.

Write two columns. One column heading will be the goal and the other column your doubts about manifesting the goal.

(Goal)   **Doubts**

2. Take each doubt and experience it fully in your body. Embrace the doubt and any resistance you may have about experiencing the doubt, until it's lost its charge and dissolves away. Many times, all you have to do is feel the doubt or belief in your body, breathe deep connected breaths and it will fade away.

Awareness Exercise

The Awareness Exercise is a very powerful tool. The exercise will assist you in achieving awareness and will help neutralize your intense dislikes. An extreme of any kind may cause you to attract what you are resisting. You will know it is an extreme by the intensity of the charge you receive on the subject. Try not to analyze each item, instead let the experience, issue or people simply pop up into your awareness.

INSTRUCTIONS

Using a separate sheet of paper create a list of everything in your life you are **resisting**. For example, make a list of things you intensely distaste or dislike.

Then, on another sheet of paper, make a list of events or experiences you **fear** will occur in your life and in the world.

After you finish your lists you will realize what you are creating in your universe. How do you change these feelings? You have just taken the first step. Gaining an awareness of the contents of your consciousness will give you the many answers you have been in search of for so long. Be aware these acts of resistance and feelings of fear are coming from your conscious and unconscious mind. You would be better served to dissolve these episodes of resistance.

About the Author

Theresa Dale is a renowned healer and educator with over 15 years of experience in helping thousands of patients transform their personal beliefs from illness into wellness. Dr. Dale possesses the profound ability to guide you through your labyrinth of beliefs, to the core within yourself that is the source of all experience. Dr. Dale's training includes a wide variety of transformational technologies, her own personal healing experiences and her inexhaustible energy and devotion to transforming mass consciousness. This training qualifies her to lead you to your own discovery of the highest state of your consciousness, ultimately empowering you to know and trust yourself as the source of all you create. Dr. Dale acknowledges that the emotional component of an illness needs to be recognized and released before a permanent health change can be achieved.

Dr. Dale enthusiastically sought out self-healing technologies at the age of 22 when she was faced with a serious diagnosis of a uterine tumor. By following her intuition and taking responsibility for this health issue, she applied the knowledge she acquired and cured herself within six months. From that moment on, her quest to explore how and why disease manifests, led her to the invention of new complementary medical technologies.

She has researched and formulated Neuro-Emotional Remedies™, which are high potency homeopathic remedies designed to release identities, their beliefs, and their emotional components. In addition, Dr. Dale has developed a laser-like system of diagnosis, NeuroPhysical Reprogramming™, allowing the health practitioner to locate the precise organ, gland, or area of the body where identities, beliefs, and emotions are stored, causing illness. She researched and personally instructs The Wellness Courses I and II - a California vocational school. Another self-healing technology that has already helped thousands of people is her Music Therapy ("5 Element Healing" and "Synchrony") and The Meta-Wellness Home Study Program.

Dr. Dale holds a Ph.D. in Naturopathic Sciences, is a board certified Naturopathic Doctor, a Certified Clinical Nutritionist, and a Certified Advanced Clinical Transpersonal Hypnotherapist. Special studies in Nutrition, Clinical

Kinesiology, Physics, Electro-Acupuncture, Homeopathy, and Electromagnetic Fields have taken her around the world: from the Hans Brugemann Institute in Germany, through Europe, South Africa and India.

Throughout her career Dr. Dale has had an active relationship with the media. She has produced and hosted, **"Health Network"** (Cable TV), both nationally and regionally in Texas and Southern California. Awards include ACTV honors for her series "Health Network", which has been running for over 10 years, and is currently produced in Los Angeles. She has been interviewed on national television's "Alive & Wellness" , CNBC, and the "Leeza Gibbons Show" (NBC). Her articles have been published in major publications.

Dr. Theresa Dales' Meta-Wellness
Self-Healing and Educational Catalog

Self-Healing Program

PRICE

The Meta-Wellness Home Study Program $350.00
The **only** complete self-healing "tool kit" on the planet today.
 Please send instructional video on the efficacy of this program   5.00
(The $5.00 charge will be applied to your purchase.)

Books:
   "Transform Your Emotional DNA" $19.95
Biotic Mac Cookbook(No dairy or meat, low fat) $10.00

Music Therapy
Part I "5 Element Healing" compact disc $16.95
Part II "Synchrony" compact disc $16.95

Audio Cassettes
 "The Nature of Health" (1 hr.) Radio Interview - KCEO 12/95 $15.00

I would like to order the products indicated above.

       Add $5.00 shipping & handling _____

       Residents of CA. Add 8.25% tax_____.

       Add $10.00 for 2nd day UPS.   _____

            TOTAL   _____

Name_____Phone_____

Address_____City_____State____Zip_____

Credit Card (Master Card and Visa Only) _____ Exp._____

Your order will be shipped in 5 to 7 working days.

Mail Order to: The Wellness Center for Research and Education, Inc.
                13050 San Vicente Blvd. #107
                Los Angeles, CA 90049
Phone in Order: 310-656-7117 or Fax Order to: 310-656-7112